Complete Soccer Handbook

Complete Soccer Handbook

Alan E. Maher

Parker Publishing Company, Inc.
West Nyack, N.Y.

© 1983, by

PARKER PUBLISHING COMPANY, INC.

West Nyack, N.Y.

Library of Congress Cataloging in Publication Data
Maher, Alan E.
  Complete soccer handbook.

  Includes index.
  1. Soccer—Coaching.   2. Soccer—Training.   3. Soccer
—Netherlands. I. Title.
GV943.8.M29 1983   796.334   83-2278
ISBN 0-13-163386-4

Printed in the United States of America

ALAN MAHER has been a thorough student and proponent of the Dutch methods of coaching and teaching soccer. Through several years of close contact with the Dutch, Mr. Maher is completely familiar with their methods. I am certain that his book, the *Complete Soccer Handbook,* will be extremely useful to coaches of all levels of soccer, from grade school through college, from youth to senior soccer clubs, for men and for women. Having spent two weeks myself at a Dutch coaching course, I can attest to the validity of their methods. I recommend Alan Maher's book to anyone interested in increasing his or her knowledge of the sport of soccer and of the various training and coaching methods.

TOM GRIFFITH
Head Soccer Coach
Dartmouth College

Dedication

To my family—my wife Angela, and my children Chris and Angel—for their patience and understanding, and the joy that they have brought to my life.

Why This Handbook Was Written

RINUS MICHELS is a world renowned Dutch soccer coach. He coached the famous Dutch team in the 1974 World Cup. He coached the Los Angeles Aztecs, and now coaches F. C. Cologne.

The last time that I spoke to Michels he mentioned the gap in soccer ability between the American player and the European player. Michels felt that the gap is widening; the European player is getting better and the American player remains the same.

Some ways that European players are better include:

1. *Technique*. European players are exposed to a greater variation of options of what to do with the ball. Also, there is more functional conditional training. That is, they are more adept at working with the ball for longer periods of time.

2. *Teamwork*. The players of Europe are better trained to work together. They are better at *anticipating* what a teammate will do; they are less inclined to "go it alone."

3. *Numerical superiority*. This is achieved and maintained with meticulous practice in a small space and with the pressure of opposition. The "game situation" is at the heart of each practice.

4. *Tactics*. These are directly taught to European players. They learn what they can expect from their opponents; they learn what electives they have available. Nothing is left to chance.

Michels concluded by saying that he feared that American soccer is fifteen years away from being truly competitive with the rest of the world.

The purpose of this handbook is to introduce to the American soccer coach the training techniques that are being used to develop the European player.

In order to help create this handbook, I studied with the national staff of the Royal Dutch Football Association (K.N.V.B.) at Zeist,

Holland in 1978 and 1980. Since then I have continued to correspond with various members of the national staff to keep abreast of what is happening in Europe.

In developing this handbook my obvious frame of reference is Dutch, but on a wider scale it could correctly be called Continental or European. Within the continent of Europe, soccer is most fluid. Coaches and players move from country to country. Training techniques are observed, critiqued and imitated. Games between countries' teams and clubs are as common as between states in America.

This handbook then is an accumulation of what I saw and what I learned.

How This Handbook Will Help You

This handbook is designed to cover the four major areas mentioned above: techniques, team work, numerical superiority, and tactics. Each section is sequential and developmental, and should be studied in some detail before the handbook is used.

Section I reviews *technique* with new drills that place fresh emphasis on the basics of passing and trapping. Also, the techniques of faking and feinting are presented in clear detail to help you teach your players these often neglected skills.

Section II covers *combination drills,* which are essential to playing modern soccer. Included are drills in wall passing, the give-and-go, and takeovers from dribbling. This section concludes with finishing combinations; no practice session is complete without a drill that provides the players an opportunity to take shots on goal.

Section III focuses on drills that stress the concept of *numerical superiority.* As the players become accustomed to establishing numerical superiority, the position-play of the players without the ball is emphasized. Then pressure is increased by adding more defenders.

Section IV covers *tactical aspects* of the game. Included are such topics as the offside trap, set plays, organizing practice sessions, and systems of play. The final chapter covers the technique of match-analysis, which is an invaluable aid in scouting an opposing team. Also, match-analysis is a way of helping you analyze the formation and movement of an opposing team during a game.

The modern game of soccer, as played in Europe, is a fluid game with players overlapping, switching, and running predetermined patterns. As such, the training emphasis in this handbook is on basic movements with the ball and meaningful position near the player with the ball. The role of players by position such as wing or fullback yields to more basic roles: when a given team has the ball all eleven players are on the attack; when the ball is lost all eleven players defend.

Successful coaches must learn to use a variety of drills and small aside games to develop an effective training program. The basics of soccer can be taught only through a sequence of drills that are presented in a meaningful format.

Dutch Soccer is based on several simple principles. The last three World Cup Tournaments seem to confirm these principles. They are:

1. Good soccer is achieved by going "back to basics." More drill work is needed in the basics to prepare for the game.

2. Winning soccer is achieved by a buildup from the defensive third to the attacking third of the field. The buildup begins slowly and safely and often ends with rapid risk-taking.

3. The Dutch believe that *pace* is a vital concept in playing soccer. While the Bulgarians play at a slow, deliberate speed, and the English play at top speed, the Dutch mix the speed. Any set pace becomes highly predictable and more easily defended. Preparation is simple if the opponent is highly predictable. The change of pace controls the game, and the men without the ball must respond to the change of pace to control the game. Since most players do *not* have the ball, it must follow that the men without the ball can control the game by the pace of their movement.

4. Players must be allowed *freedom*. Once players have learned a variety of skills, they must be free to select from this variety. Players must grow and develop until they reach a point where they can choose. This freedom of choice is a major principle that reflects even a cultural attitude. Thus, Dutch soccer is a reflection of Dutch society.

Symbols used in the diagrams

X = Attacking player

〰〰〰➤ = Player moving with ball

───➤ = Movement of the ball alone

○ = Defending player

------➤ = Player moving without ball

Acknowledgments

I am indebted to the national staff of the Royal Dutch Football Association (K.N.V.B.) for taking me light years ahead in understanding the real game of soccer. In particular, I would like to thank Rob Baan of the K.N.V.B. for his continued support and help since my first visit with the national staff.

I would also like to thank Gordon Bradley and Hubert Vogelsinger for their infectious enthusiasm of the game, and Chris Sweeney and Bob Wernersbach for their generous support. Finally, I must acknowledge my indebtedness to "Pat" McComiskey, who is truly "Mr. Soccer" on Long Island, and Hank van Weeren, who has been my loyal "Dutch Connection."

Contents

11

Section I

Technique

Chapter One

Dribbling–Turning–Feinting

IN SOCCER, there are few moments more exciting than watching the ball being passed into space in the penalty area, then met by an attacker who controls the ball, beats a defender and scores! It is in this moment that the individual player face the ultimate test: the willingness to take the ball to an opponent and beat him. All the drama and excitement of soccer boils down to this moment.

Today's soccer player must be well trained to meet this test. He must be prepared to make the most of this moment when it appears.

He must be able to control the ball:

1. Dribbling
2. Turning
3. Feinting

The training program begins with dribbling, and to this is added turning and feinting. As such, the training program begins where the tactical game ends, with a single player and the ball facing his immediate opponent.

Dribbling in Free Space

1. Each player begins with a ball and dribbles the length of the field. Every time a player dribbles the length of the field, a different

part of the foot should be used so that the player has a chance to feel and experience different ways of dribbling. Emphasize using both feet in dribbling. The inside of the foot and the outside of the foot should be used. For a more forceful driving of the ball, the instep should be used. Caution your players to look up.

2. *Looking up* is a practice that can be reinforced by shadow dribbling. The player with the ball follows the movement of a playmate without a ball. Both players stop on signal. The player without the ball spreads his legs and the other player passes the ball between his legs. Then the roles are reversed and the drill continues.

3. Now two players dribble in a figure-eight circuit. Two poles about 15 yards apart can mark the area to be covered, or two resting players can act as markers. As the players meet in the middle, they will be forced to look up to avoid colliding as they pass. See Diagram 1-1.

Diagram 1-1

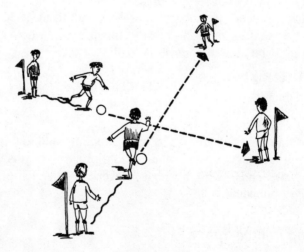

Diagram 1-2

4. Again, to force the players to look up, the players can run a crisscross pattern. The player with the ball dribbles to a teammate who then dribbles in the opposite direction. Each group has three players and one ball. See Diagram 1-2.

5. From midfield, the players should dribble one at a time at the goal and shoot when entering the penalty area. When this drill is running well, a defender should be placed in front of the goal to force the one-on-one situation.

Relay Races

Because players like competition, relay races and similar competitive games add interest to the drills.

1. Divide the team into two or more groups that dribble around a pole, as in Diagram 1-3.

Diagram 1-3

2. The same teams can run a slalom race around a series of poles.

3. As a variation, both teams can run around the same pole to run a relay race.

4. The slalom relay race can be run using standing players instead of poles. If four teams are used, two act as poles, while two race. Then the positions are reversed.

Dribbling and Turning

Arrange the players in groups of two in a circle at least 20 yards in diameter (Diagram 1-4).

Diagram 1-4

The front player in each group of two has the ball. The center of the circle is marked with a cone or similar object. In the drills that follow, the player is to dribble to the center of the circle, turn, dribble to the teammate, turn, dribble to the center, turn, dribble and pass off to the teammate. That is, he dribbles four laps with turns, then passes to his teammate who does the same thing.

Instruct your players to dribble slowly at first, with the ball under complete control. On the turn, they must move suddenly, *explode*, and carry the ball in the opposite direction. The key to these drills is the sudden explosive turns. This is the *Dutch change of pace*.

1. Dribble to the center, place the right foot on the ball and pull the ball back with the sole of the foot. Pivot on the other foot and dribble back.

2. Do the same drill, but turn with the sole of the left foot.

3. Dribble to the center and pull the ball back with the outside of the right foot; turn and dribble back.

4. Dribble to the middle and turn with the outside of the left foot.

5. Dribble to the center, and with the ball outside the left foot, cross over with the right foot and chop the ball in the reverse direction with the instep of the right foot. Turn and dribble back.

6. Cross over with the left foot and chop the ball back.

7. Dribble to the center and suddenly push the ball in the opposite direction with the inside of the right foot. Turn and dribble back.

8. Finally, push the ball in reverse with the left foot. As the above drills are being run, the size of the circle can gradually be increased, until the diameter is 40 yards. In addition to technique, the drills now also stress conditioning.

9. When all of the above variations have been executed successfully, the players should be allowed to have a free choice of how they want to turn with the ball, and with either foot. They should be encouraged to use a variety of turns.

10. With the circle now 40 yards wide, the players can dribble to the opposite side, turn and dribble back. With half the players dribbling to the center at the same time, there will be trouble getting through the center and on to the other side.

The players will quickly learn to look up, and also vary the pace of the dribbling to prevent losing the ball in "heavy traffic." As mentioned before, the players can be told what kind of turn to make. Then the players can be given the freedom to make any turn.

11. As a final circle drill, the players can dribble to the opposite side, turn, and pass in the air to their waiting teammate. Then the teammate can execute the same drill.

Feinting

The team should be organized in two lines of players. The player with the ball faces a teammate about 15 yards away. For each drill the player with the ball dribbles to the teammate, makes a feint, dribbles by the player, and beyond for about 12 yards, turns, and dribbles back to repeat the feint. Then the players reverse roles. Initially, the player without the ball simply stands still acting as a passive defender. The key to these drills is to make a sudden move—the feint—to cause a reaction by the defender.

1. The player with the ball dribbles to the defender and fakes a kick with the right foot. This will cause the defender to react by moving to *his* right. Then, using the outside of the right foot or the inside of the left foot, the dribbler carries the ball around the defender's left side. See Diagrams 1-5A and 1-5B.

The motion of the false kick must be distinct and separate from the next move that carries the ball around the defender 1-2. This can be seen by not carrying the ball too close to the defender for the feint.

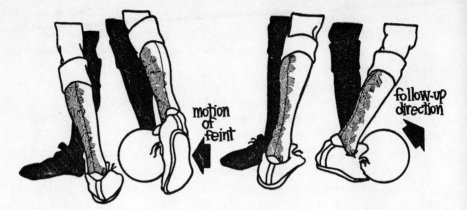

Diagram 1-5A

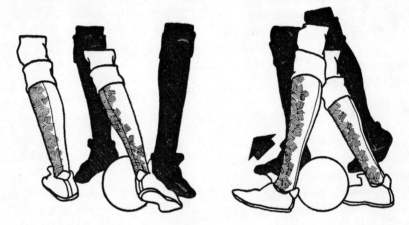

Diagram 1-5B

When the ball is carried too close to the defender, there is a tendency to make the two moves one smooth action.

2. The same fake shot is taken, but this time with the left foot, and the ball is carried around the defender's right side.

3. The dribbler carries the ball to the defender, makes a quarter turn, and carries the ball beyond him. See Diagram 1-5B.

4. The same drill is run with a quarter turn to the other side. In the quarter turn, the body is used to screen the ball from the defender.

5. The player with the ball dribbles to the defender, passes the

ball between his legs, runs behind the defender and picks up the ball to continue dribbling. The trick for this feint is to dribble directly at the near shin bone and at the last moment push the ball between the legs. See Diagram 1-6A.

The defender must be passive to allow a successful execution of this feint. The feint must be allowed to take place.

Diagram 1-6A

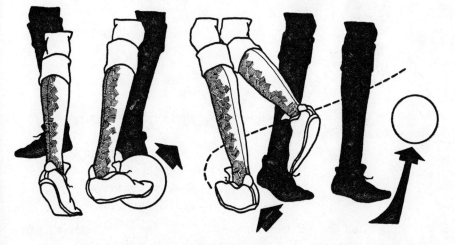

Diagram 1-6B

6. The same fake is now executed with the opposite foot carrying the ball to the other leg.

7. The player with the ball dribbles to the defender, passes around one side and runs around the other to continue the dribble. The key to this feint is to dribble face on, near leg to near leg, and then pass. See Diagram 1-6B.

8. The same feint is tried to the opposite side. In all cases, the dribble should be slow and sure until the players have developed confidence and ability.

9. The final feint is the step-over. The player fakes a push pass in one direction while the ball is really passed to the opposite side. In Diagram 1-7, the player begins with a motion to push pass the ball with the inside of the right foot. However, instead of striking the ball, the foot is carried over the ball in a sudden movement causing the defender to move in the wrong direction. Before the defender can recover, the ball is passed by him with the outside of the same foot. This movement should be tried with each foot. For the fake to be effective, the ball must be in front of the dribbler, but close enough to be under control at all times.

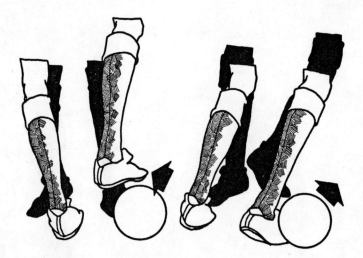

Diagram 1-7

10. After the step-over has been learned, the players can practice the double step-over. With this variation the player feints the push with

one foot, returns the foot to the original place, and then makes a second step-over with the other foot. This second step-over is followed by a pass forward. The first step-over is made in a circular motion for the foot to return to the original place.

The Role of the Defender

During all of the above variations, the player acting as the defender is asked to stand, feet apart, in a passive manner. After the player with the ball is skillful at dribbling and feinting, the defender can be activated.

The movement of the defender will determine the movement of the dribbler. If the defender moves forward rapidly at the dribbler, then the dribbler must move slowly. Speed causes mistakes. The slow movement of the dribbler will give the defender the opportunity to make the first mistake.

If the defender falls backward, the dribbler should move forward, *rapidly.* This will allow the dribbler to move through the *space* that is being vacated by the defender. The second purpose is to force the defender to mark the dribbler. Dribblers can fake defenders, not space. Dribblers must try to get *behind* defenders. That movement is what makes the player with the ball dangerous. The Dutch say, "Seek the defender; find him!"

First the defenders should be instructed to move forward. When the dribblers are able to feint and pass the defender in this situation, then the defenders should be instructed to fall back. Finally, the defender is free to move forward or backward.

After practice in dribbling turning and feinting, the players can be paired for some games of one-on-one. The one-on-one duel will be examined in detail in Chapter Three.

Chapter Two

Passing and Trapping

ONCE A PLAYER is able to dribble, turn and feint with the ball, he is ready to begin work with a teammate. The basic relationship with a teammate is through passing and trapping.

Passing and trapping techniques are best learned in a developmental sequence. The drills that follow are in a systematic sequence that initially allows for passing and trapping only. Then one player is allowed movement. After both players move simultaneously, a defender is introduced. This chapter concludes with drills for three players. Units of three create variations that will help to sustain the interest of the participants. Four players with one ball may not give the individual player enough practice, so we end with groups of three.

Two Players Passing and Trapping

1. Two players stand about 15 yards apart. The motion is two steps. Trap-touch one. Pass-second touch. Both the inside of the foot and the instep should be used. Also, use both feet. Both players stand in place. See Diagram 2-1.

2. Next, one player moves in an arc from side to side. The moving player should practice receiving the ball with the inside of the foot, and then with the outside of the foot. After a short interval, the players reverse roles.

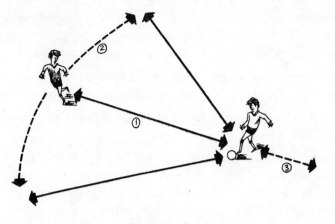

Diagram 2-1

3. Now the movement of one player is back and forth. The player moves forward to play the ball, and then moves backward until the ball is passed back to him. The movement of both the player and the ball must be slow.

4. When these two movements are executed successfully, the moving player should combine both motions . . . move to the side, pass, and move back.

5. After both players have had practice in moving, they can move alternately from side to side. This will create a more game-like situation, and will help in the conditioning of the players. Teamwork is essential, if the two are to work together successfully. As an alternative, they can dribble to the side and then pass. While this variation will eliminate the through pass to the diagonally opposite corner, it will provide for dribbling in place of running without the ball. Your trainer must decide what his purpose is.

6. Up to now the two players have been about 15 yards apart. They should now increase the distance between them. (For a full team this may require the space of half a field.) At first the ball can be played on the ground, but as the distance is increased, the ball must be played in the air with the instep if it is to go the required distance. Players must develop a natural "feel" of when push passing ends and instep passing begins.

At the same time the duties of the receiver become more exact and demanding. The player receiving the ball must position himself to protect the ball from a defender. Even in drillwork without a defender the receiver must be aware of his role—*protect the ball*. Then the pace must be changed suddenly, without warning, as though rapidly moving from a defender. Therefore, the receiver must be aware of three factors:

a. The speed of the pass—and moving to control that pass
b. Placing his body to protect the ball from a defender
c. The change of pace after the ball is controlled to carry it *away* from the defender

Never allow the players to develop lazy habits in controlling the ball just because the drills are practice and are not "real" games.

7. The passing groups of two should now practice on half a field. Six groups of two should pass back and forth. Pressure can be given by introducing four players to the field to act as defenders. The defenders should roam around trying to steal the ball from the pairs who are interpassing. The presence of the defenders will put game-like pressure on the passing pairs. This will reinforce the concepts of:

a. Speed of passing
b. Protecting the ball
c. Change of pace after controlling the pass

As the defenders intercept the ball, they should change place with the passer or with the last player to touch the ball. Obviously no more than one defender should try to interrupt the passing exchange of two players. The passing players will soon find the range of their passing abilities; they will find out how close they can get without the constant presence of a defender; they will find out how far away from each other they can move without allowing the defender to beat the pass receiver to the ball. With six groups interpassing and only four defenders, there must be aggressive movement by the defenders. If the total number of groups is more or less than sixteen, a similar ratio should be maintained of more passing groups than defenders.

8. As a final two-man drill, all the players are assembled in groups of two on one-half a field. The players pass slowly, moving around the field. Then as a pair of players reach the midfield circle, they should suddenly carry the ball to the opposite end of the field. This move must be sudden and the ball must be passed back and forth quickly. Only one pair at a time should attack the opposite goal, but all the pairs should move downfield in rotation. After attacking the goal the pair moves off the field and returns to the first half to begin passing again.

There are two major objectives that can be achieved by this drill.

First, the slow passing followed by the sudden burst of speed from midfield simulates the concept of the build-up, where slow, safe passing in the first third of the field is followed by the sudden, rapid attack on goal. The concept of the change of pace can also be practiced in this drill.

Second, as the two players move from the center circle to attack the goal, they can interpass in a predetermined pattern. These patterns will be discussed in detail in the next section.

When the sudden attack on goal is being run successfully, a defender can be stationed in front of the goal. (The roaming defenders can also be reintroduced at the first end.) Now the attack on goal is a 2 v 1 situation. Then a center forward can be added to create a 3 v 1 situation. Finally, a sweeper is added to create a 3 v 2 attack on goal.

A center forward can be stationed downfield. He must check in/check out on the defender to keep open for a pass from the advancing pair with the ball. This will create a 3 v 1 situation.

When this drill variation is running well, a sweeper can be added. Now the ratio will be 3 v 2, which will give the attackers game-like pressure. The defenders must be alert as wave after wave of passing pairs attack the goal.

Additional pressure can be created by giving the attackers a set time in which to attack the goal. For example, they can be allowed 20 seconds to score or shoot after crossing into the penalty area.

The attackers must be given time and practice to create a rhythm. Once a rhythm is established, restraints must be established to disturb that rhythm. There are many restraints that can be introduced:

    a. An additional defender can be introduced
    b. A time frame can be added—such as 20 seconds
    c. Defenders can move from 50 percent pressure to 100 percent pressure
    d. Passing can be restricted—two touch, then one touch
    e. Movement can be restricted—the passer must run an overlap

None of the above restraints can be introduced until the players have experienced success with a given drill. Initial adjustments must be made to make the drills work. Then pressure can be applied.

Two-Player Pass-Run Combinations

There are a series of simple drills practiced in Germany and Holland that involve two or three players. They establish a pattern of passing and running that is then sustained over a given distance. There are several important reasons for running these drills.

1. By having a small unit of two or three work together, the participants learn to develop teamwork; they learn to be unselfish in passing; they run to support the man with the ball.

2. Basic technique is reinforced. Trapping and passing on the move are difficult techniques that require constant practice.

3. Having the ball moved within an established pattern of passing and running helps a team to establish a rhythm or flow. This helps a team to control the ball and, in turn, control the game itself. Since only one player at a time can control the ball, the movement of the remaining attackers controls the pace, and the pace or variations of the pace control the game. It is assumed that the team that controls the game normally wins the game.

4. Various patterns and rhythms with the ball help to change the pace of the game. The Dutch and the Germans believe that the pace must be changed during the game, and the control of the pace is the control of the game.

5. Sudden movement by a player is a silent signal that calls for the ball. Players must learn to recognize this movement and respond to it.

6. Teams must learn to avoid becoming predictable to their opponents. But they must be able to predict teammates' movements.

Passing and running in a pattern will help players to predict each other's movements.

In Diagram 2-2, player X_1 begins dribbling with the ball. His teammate is about 10 yards away running even with him. Suddenly X_2 bursts ahead, signaling that he wants the ball. Player X_1 passes to X_2 and catches up to run even with X_2, who traps the ball and begins to dribble ahead. When player X_1 wants the ball, he signals this message by bursting ahead of X_2. Player X_2 responds by passing the ball to X_1. Now the pattern is established—pass-touch-dribble-pass again. The pass can be in front of or behind the running teammate. The trainer must control where the pass is played. As the player receives the ball, he must bring it under control and slow down the pace.

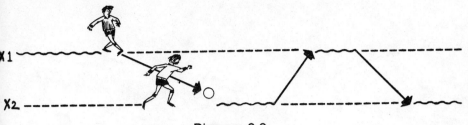

Diagram 2-2

Method:

1. All groups can start from the same spot, one after the other. As an example, they can run from goal line to goal line. After they finish, they can practice passing in place while they wait for the other groups to finish. Then they can run in the reverse direction.

2. The distance covered can vary. Some groups can start at the goal line, others at the 18-yard line, and others at midfield.

3. The pace can be constant from beginning to end.

4. The pace can change. Normally, the change is from slow to fast.

5. The passing can be two-touch or one-touch.

6. The drill can end with a shot on goal.

7. If a shot is to be taken, a defender can be added in front of the goal.

Two-man combinations:

Below are variations of two-man combinations. It is not necessary to try every combination. The trainer must consider what purpose is to be served.

1. *The zigzag:* This is the combination, in which each player runs straight and lead passes to his teammate.

2. *The lead-square:* In this variation, one player always lead passes, while the other always square passes.

3. *Change places:* This time the first player makes a lead pass and follows the pass. His teammate traps and controls the ball and dribbles to take over the first player's place.

4. *Takeover:* Instead of passing, the first player dribbles toward his teammate. As they meet, the second player takes over the ball and dribbles back. See Diagram 2-3.

Diagram 2-3

5. In a final two-man combination the takeover is from the rear to the front. Player X_1 passes downfield to X_2 who dribbles away from the goal. In Diagram 2-4, Player X_1 runs in the direction of his pass overtaking the spot where X_2 received the pass.

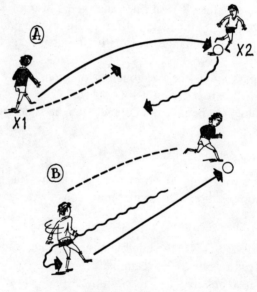

Diagram 2-4

Three Players Passing and Trapping

The practice of passing and trapping can also be done with groups of three players.

1. Three players form a triangle and trap/pass first clockwise and then reverse direction.

2. The three players can now move in their corners. They can move back and forth as in the two-man drills. Then they can move back and forth.

3. The players pass the ball in one direction and overlap the player that is passed to. Then the direction is reversed. See Diagram 2-5.

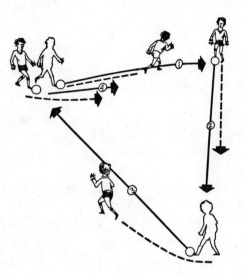

Diagram 2-5

4. As a variation for passing and trapping, the groups of three can move into an open area. Each time the ball is passed, the players must position themselves left and right of the player with the ball. Players must learn to support the man with the ball. Inexperienced players have a tendency either to stand and watch the ball, or to turn their backs and run away. The player with the ball has maximum support if he can pass to the left or to the right.

Each pass will force players to move to be in proper support position to the left and right of the ball. The player who passed the ball begins to support his teammate if he moves in the direction of his pass ... moving toward the receiver of the pass.

5. For a rapidly-paced drill, three players are stationed in a line about 15 yards long (Diagram 2-6).

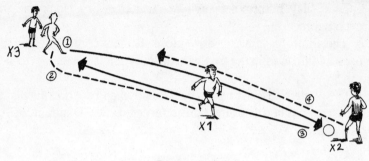

Diagram 2-6

Player X_1 passes to X_2 and runs to take his place. When X_2 receives the ball, he passes to X_3 and takes his place. The rotation continues.

This simple drill teaches the passing player to move in the direction of the ball for support, and to overlap a position. The players can initially two-touch, and then one-touch. Both the left foot and the right foot should be used.

6. As a variation, two lines can play crisscross. It is probably best that the player with the ball dribbles halfway, looking up, and passes the final half of the distance. For this reason the distance between the players should be increased. See Diagram 2-7.

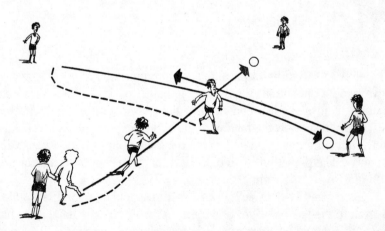

Diagram 2-7

This is an excellent drill to teach pass/trapping and dribbling. The intersection will be busy with players and balls making the participants more alert and perceptive. The movement is also good for conditioning.

7. A 15-yard-by-15-yard grid can also be used by three players to give practice in passing/trapping and forcing movement following a pass.

In Diagram 2-8, player X_2 turns and lead passes to X_1. Player X_2 must turn away from the side that X_1 passes him on. This kind of turn will be on the defender's blind side. This is a most effective combination.

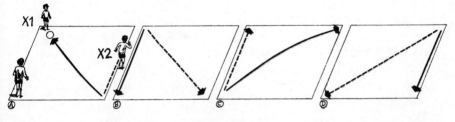

Diagram 2-8

Other combinations can be designated by the trainer. As an example, following the takeover combination, the two players can run a fake takeover combination.

Three-Player Passing-Running Patterns

We will give three examples of pass-run combinations that can be run with three players. The possibility of combinations is much higher than those with two men. The trainer must be guided by his individual purpose. The objectives for these drills are the same as for the two-man combinations covered earlier.

1. The first drill uses the central player to control the pace by his lead passes.

In Diagram 2-9, Player X_2 lead passes to his left. Then player X_1 dribbles briefly, and square passes to the outside right player X_3. This player backpasses to X_2 who controls the ball, dribbles briefly and starts the pattern again.

The players can carry this pattern for a distance and then change places so that all have an opportunity to practice each position.

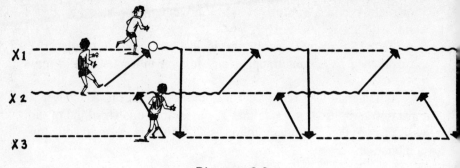

Diagram 2-9

2. The second combination is similar. The center player again begins with a lead pass. Now the outside player square passes to the central player.

In Diagram 2-10, player X_2 begins with a lead pass to X_1 who controls the ball, dribbles briefly, and square passes back to X_2. Now X_2 lead passes to the other side. Player X_3 controls the ball, dribbles and square passes into X_2. Player X_2 dribbles and starts the pattern again with a lead pass to his left.

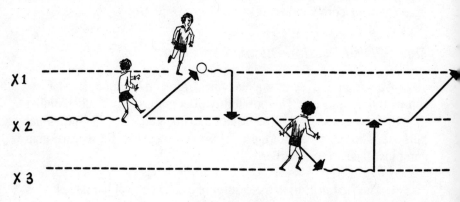

Diagram 2-10

3. This final drill is started by an outside player, and the pace is very rapid.

In Diagram 2-11, player X_1 dribbles briefly and lead passes to X_2, who dribbles briefly and lead passes to X_3. Player X_3 dribbles and lead passes to X_2 to start the ball back in the other direction. Now X_2

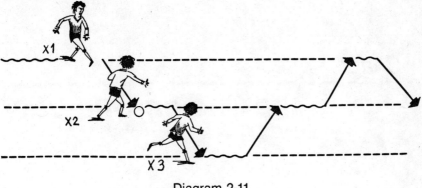

Diagram 2-11

dribbles and lead passes to X_1, where the ball started. After a brief dribble, player X_1 starts again with a lead pass to X_2.

There are many more patterns that can be created. By simply introducing overlapping, the combination becomes more complex and challenging.

Most players like to run these patterns. They help to develop technique and teamwork. Also, they are hidden conditioning drills. As a result, players will tire quickly, but their interests can be sustained by ending with a shot on goal. Add a defender for a game-like situation.

Chapter Three

The One-on-One-Duel

ONCE A PLAYER has learned how to dribble, turn feint, pass and trap, he is ready to take the ultimate test ... the one-on-one duel. Sooner or later every soccer player must face this test, in which the player with the ball is challenged by an opposing defender.

You can introduce a series of drills or mini-games to help your players prepare for this ultimate test. But beyond that, there are specified objectives that can be identified and met in these mini-games. These objectives must be more defined than just having the defender oppose the attacker with the ball. What are these objectives? How are they learned and reinforced by practicing the one-on-one duel?

Purpose

The most obvious purpose of the duel is to provide practice in having a player dribble, turn, and feint with the ball. More than that, the dribbler must try to get behind the immediate defender; once a defender is passed, the dribbler is much more dangerous.

Less obvious an objective is having the dribbler slide just to the side of a defender to gain the half-step needed for a shot on goal. The defender's task in such a situation is to force the attacker so far to the sideline that the shooting angle is poor or nonexistent. The dribbler then must quickly gain the half-step while a good shooting angle is still available.

Since an objective of the dribbler is to maintain ball possession, the dribbler must become adept at screening the ball from the defender. The abilities to dribble, turn, and feint are aids in screening the ball and maintaining ball control.

This whole process will help the dribbler to focus his attention on the relative position of his teammates, opponents, the goal, and the ball. Dribblers must develop a wide field of vision. They must also learn to sense or feel where the ball is when it is not in a direct line of vision. The introduction of an opponent makes this task more difficult, and the situation more game-like. Obviously, practice is most meaningful when it most closely resembles an actual game.

Defender's Role

For the defender, the prime objective is to prevent penetration with the ball. Defenders often try to gain possession of the ball when all they need to do is turn aside the attacker to a poor shooting position. Defenders should not try to regain possession of the ball until they know that they have support of their teammates. If a defender is passed by the attacker with the ball, he has allowed the attacker to become more dangerous.

When support of teammates is evident, the defender can try to tackle the ball. In the absence of a real support player, the defender can be instructed by the coach as to when he can or cannot tackle an opponent. Players should be instructed in how to execute the block tackle and the slide tackle.

One other form of body contact is the shoulder charge. This move is best reviewed with current soccer law and the current interpretation of the local referees. Local enforcement of the shoulder charge is often an all-important factor as to whether or not it should be tried.

Overall Objectives

The final objectives of running one-on-one drills are twofold:

1. *Fitness:* One-on-one drills call for the individual player to give 100 percent effort for periods of 30 seconds up to two minutes at a time. While this may seem like a relatively small amount of time, for the player it often proves to be most exhaustive. If players are to

respond properly, they must be in good physical condition; for those who fail to respond, persistent practice will help to develop physically fit players.

2. *Confidence:* There is a trite phrase, "Nothing succeeds like success." It has a ring of truth to it; success brings success. Players must experience the success of controlling the ball and beating a defender. Players must reach a point where they are *willing* to take the ball to a defender. It is easy to spot players who lack self-confidence. They quickly pass the ball when defenders approach. Or they carry the ball to the sideline. On occasions they dribble directly to a teammate.

Practice

Only frequent, regular practice in the duel will give players the necessary experience that is the prerequisite to confidence. It is strongly recommended that part of *each* practice be devoted to some form of one-on-one work. The drills that follow are some suggested variations. But the variety is almost endless. Coaches must adjust each drill according to local needs and conditioning.

Two players

A goal can be made of corner flags. The goalmouth should be about 2 yards wide. (Two steps will do.) Two players attack and defend the one goal. It can be attacked from either side. When the defender gains possession of the ball, he begins the attack by carrying the ball away from the goal to a starting point, such as 15 yards away. Or, he can carry the ball around a corner of the goal to attack it from the opposite side. The defender has the advantage of being able to run *through* the goalmouth. For a team of sixteen players, eight small goals can be scattered over half a playing field. See Diagram 3-1.

The players will need rest at regular intervals. After a period of time going one-on-one, they can rest by interpassing, from a standing position, for an equal period of time. The time period can first be 30 seconds, then 45 seconds, and finally one minute. The "rest" activity can vary: push passing, throw-in practice, heading, etc. Ten minutes will give five periods of one-on-one and practice in five basic techniques that need work.

For a variation, two goals can be used, about 15 yards apart. Each

Diagram 3-1

player is assigned one goal to defend and the opposite to attack. If played with intensity, this drill will quickly tire the participants.

Four players

Two players can act as goals for the drill. They should stand facing each other 10 to 15 yards apart with their legs spread and standing firmly to allow the space between their feet to serve as the goalmouth. The other two players attack in one direction and defend in the other, so that each defends one goal and attacks the opposite. After a period of work, one minute or less, rest time is given by having the active players switch with those acting as goals. As a variation, the attacking player can have a resting-goal player act as a teammate. This resting player will hold an extra ball and throw it to his teammate when the game ball is kicked out-of-bounds. The real advantage is that the drill is accelerated since there is no time-out to retrieve out-of-bounds balls.

Six players

This variation introduces an extra resting player behind and to the side of the goal player. The rotation would be from one-on-one to sideline rest behind the goal—then act as goal—and finally back to one-on-one work. If the playing area is well-marked, additional players can rest on each side. This is an excellent way to demonstrate this drill. The team can watch one group demonstrate, and if the resting players are scattered around the playing field, there will never be a loss of playing time to chase out-of-bounds balls.

Variations for any number

Two lines of players are formed facing a common goal. As an example, the two lines can begin at midfield facing a regulation goal. The coach or a neutral player begins the drill by passing the ball upfield between the two lines at the goal. When the ball is passed, the first player from each line tries to get to the ball to score a goal. Initially there will be a struggle for possession of the ball. Shoulder charges and other techniques can be tried. See Diagram 3-2.

Once the ball is in the possession of one player, the second player has no choice but to defend the goal and prevent the first player from scoring.

A second variation is to have the two players wait facing the neutral player who will pass the ball. The two waiting players may

Diagram 3-2

begin on the 18-yard line. Now the struggle has the added element of forcing the players to turn with the ball, so they can face the goal for a shot. See Diagram 3-3.

Diagram 3-3

In each of these variations the individual player must initially decide if he wants to try to get the ball or defend the goal. Practice will give him the confidence to go for the ball or defend the goal, according to the circumstances. While each player in theory has an equal chance to possess the ball, a few practices will reveal those players who are bold and willing to go to the ball.

The duel with support

A final variation introduces support for the player with the ball. Support players are stationed on each sideline, but off the playing field. They may aid the attacking player by one-touch passing the ball. This will create wall-passing situations for the attacker. The support players cannot enter onto the playing field, and they must stay even on each side with the attacker in the attacking half of the field. Thus, the supporting player helps only in the advanced part of the field. (The attacker can use his goalkeeper for support in the defensive half as in Figure 3-4.)

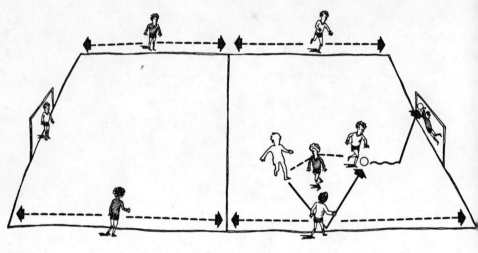

Diagram 3-4

With this variation, there is a shift in purpose and emphasis. Now the attacker is encouraged to use support in moving the ball downfield. Soccer is a team game, and players must be encouraged to use the support of teammates when it is available. In no way does this suggest that at some given point in development a player should be encouraged to pass as a preference to going one-on-one. Rather, the player should be made aware of the fact that even in challenging a defender one-on-one, the very act of challenging may free a teammate who can then receive the ball.

The more electives that the player with the ball is aware that he has, the more potentially dangerous he becomes to his opponents. This increases his *freedom* of variety in execution and reduces his *predictability* to the opposing team.

In all of the above drills the initial time period must be short ... 30 seconds or 45 seconds at most. If the drill is repeated several times, then intervals of one minute are sufficient. The final execution can be two minutes, but only after it has been tried on a few occasions.

As a final word of caution, coaches should avoid labeling players as forwards or fullbacks, attackers or defenders. Players must learn that when their team is on the attack with the ball, *all members of the team* are on the attack; when the ball is lost, *all members of the team* are on the defense. The transition from attack to defense, and back to attack must be *quick and efficient*. Many European coaches believe that the team that is quicker in the transition from attack to defense is the team that wins. This is where training pays off for the well-coached team.

Chapter Four

The Dutch System

THE DUTCH SYSTEM OF PLAY is a style that is widely admired and the subject of numerous articles. It is frequently called "the Whirl," or referred to as "Total Soccer." Sometimes the impression is given that the Dutch system is an undisciplined swirl of activity that causes confusion by opponents and spectators alike. Nothing could be further from the truth.

What is the system? How can it be recognized? What makes it work? Can it be copied? A careful explanation of the Dutch system will answer these questions and clarify the Dutch approach for the serious coach and the casual observer.

Let's begin by reviewing some of the principles of Dutch soccer that were explained in the preface:

1. The buildup from the defensive third of the field
2. Pace of the game—it must vary
3. Freedom of technical/tactical response
4. The establishment of numerical superiority near the ball

A team is placed on the field in a given *formation,* such as 4-3-3. With the 4-3-3 formation the team has four defenders (one is normally a sweeper) forming the third line. The three midfield players form the second line, and three forwards form the first line.

The system of play relates how the three lines interact and create teamwork. The Dutch system is designed to create teamwork. The

Dutch system is also designed to create a numerical advantage in each third of the field. This numerical superiority should allow the attacking team to maintain ball control and team possession as the ball is carried to the attacking end of the field. See Diagram 4-1A.

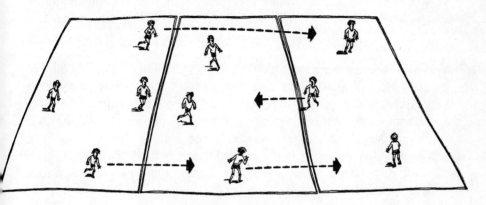

Diagram 4-1A

Consider the following example:

Team O is attacking to the left, and Team X is attacking to the right.

If Team O gains possession of the ball in their defensive third of the field, they should be able to possess and control the ball, since they have a 4-3-3 ratio of players. (See Diagram 4-1B.)

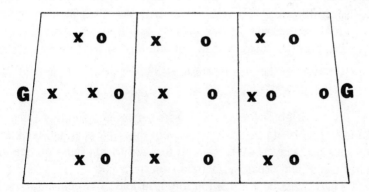

Diagram 4-1B

In order to get the ball successfully through the midfield, team O must add a player to change the ratio from 3-3 to a superior one of 4-3. This means either moving up a fullback, or pulling back a forward.

The same problem exists in the final third. Ignoring the sweeper who does not normally mark a player, the ratio is 3-3 and should be changed to 4-3 or even better 5-3. This may mean moving up two players ... perhaps a halfback and a fullback.

This, in summary, is the Dutch system of play. In the first third of the field, all passes are safe, sure passes with ample use of the goalkeeper if pressure is applied by the opponents. This is called the "building up" part of the game. The buildup continues until one player facing downfield is free to receive the ball and pass or carry it downfield. This player is often called "the window" player. It is much more difficult for a player if he must control and pass and then *turn* with the ball.

The ball actually should be passed through or over the midfield (i.e., the second line). Short passing in midfield normally spells trouble, so it is best to pass from the first third directly to the final third of the field.

The buildup ends with the ball in the final third of the field with men "coming from behind" to create the desired 5-3 ratio. Speed is of the essence. The players must be brave and take risks in going 1 v 1 with a defender.

The buildup begins with the goalkeeper. He is the key to the attack, as he is the first man on the attack when he has the ball.

In Diagram 4-2 the keeper can give the ball to #5 *if* he is not marked as he falls back toward the goal line. Player #4 can move into #5's space for a pass. If #10 moves with #4, then there is space for #3 to receive the pass.

Two points are stressed in the buildup:

1. Never get flat; that is, create a straight line across the field.
2. Get as wide as possible. Width is imperative.

As #3 dribbles forward and #5 runs upfield, there is a danger of a straight line being formed. To prevent this, #4 must fall back as #5 runs forward. Player #2 is running forward to add his presence to the midfield line and create numerical superiority (4 v 3).

There must be a transition into midfield. The center forward can

Diagram 4-2

drop back to help. Then the superiority is 5 v 3. Now speed is essential. If the ball stays too long at midfield, the odds will be equalized.

Because of the danger that can be created at midfield, the buildup with the fullbacks and goalkeeper is followed by a breakout with the ball being carried or passed *through* midfield to the forwards. While the theory is to create numerical superiority in each third of the field, in actual practice the players must always try to pass from the defensive third to the attacking third. For this reason, the midfield players do not spread out across the field in an attempt to "control" midfield. Instead, the midfield players are instructed to form a triangle creating passing lanes from the outside fullbacks to the wing attackers.

Practice in the buildup is simple. The four fullbacks and goalkeeper use half a field to keep the ball from three forwards who act as defenders. The drill ends with the ball being passed to an unmarked (window) man who begins the breakout.

The breakout typically begins when the stopper or centrally located player dribbles upfield, through space, finally passing when he is challenged. The alternative is to pass the ball to a player near the touchline, who is looking upfield. He can pass or carry the ball forward, depending on the movement of the opposition.

At this point a center forward can be added at the opposite end to receive the breakout pass. A marking defender is also added. The nearest breakout player runs forward to support the center forward and create a 2 v 1 situation.

As a final step a sweeper is added against the center forward. Now two players must run forward to create 3 v 2 odds.

Suppose that the buildup fails because all players in the defensive third are being marked? In that case, the ball should be returned to the goalkeeper for a long punt upfield. Obviously, if all the defensive players are being marked, the forwards will have an easier time attacking the goal. Just get the ball up to them.

The Dutch Method of Attacking the Goal

The common method of attack is to try to dribble directly at the goal and shoot, even if the angle is bad. Otherwise, carry the ball to the corner and cross to the middle for a header.

The Dutch say to carry the ball directly to the goal line and then pass in at a back angle. The advantages to this are:

1. No one is offside on the pass
2. The ball is moved *away* from the goalkeeper
3. The ball is moved into a more central position for better shooting

Three players should be positioned for this back-centering pass:

   a. Near post
   b. Far post (near the 6-yard line)
   c. At the 18-yard line

The centering pass can be in the air or on the ground, but on the ground is better. Fullbacks will often turn to face this ball. If they try to clear it, the result may end up as a corner kick.

Unselfish passing is the essential key. The Germans take very strong shots at goal. The Dutch do not seem to *need* a strong shot with this centering pass. We have seen the ball walked into the goal.

Future drill work in this manual will stress:

1. Slow, safe buildup.
2. Long, deep, penetrating passes from the first third (defensive), to the final third (attacking) of the field.
3. Players running from behind to forward positions to support the attack and reverse ratios from 1 v 2 to 3 v 2, etc. With a player "coming from behind," there must be an element of surprise ... or there should be.
4. Patterns of passing/running identified and practiced to develop smooth movement on the field of play.

Section II

Combination Drills

THE FIRST SECTION of this manual emphasized the individual player and his basic skills needed. We began with dribbling and developed to players working together to practice passing and trapping.

While the players worked in groups of two or three at a time, the emphasis was placed on one player, or a series of players *in sequence:* first a player passes a ball; then the player receives the ball; then the player passes the ball. The activity is learned in a serial fashion.

In this section the players must learn to work together. While one player has the ball, a teammate moves to a position of support. The support player must anticipate the movement of the ball and what will follow after the first pass.

Players must now work more in coordination with each other in a variety of *combinations* of pass/run, pass/pass patterns. Anticipation and timing become more critical to the success of the drill. Such drills are rightfully called *combination* drills.

This section will stress two-man drills as they are the most basic. A sample of a three-man drill will follow, and

53

the section ends with these drills being combined with a finishing drill—shooting.

One possible two-man combination has been omitted. The takeover combination is basically a dribbling exercise, and it will be detailed in the section covering 2 v 1 variations.

These combinations of two or three men working together are essential for the success of any modern team. Players must be able to *recognize* and execute the wall pass, the give-and-go, the up-back-and-through, as well as the takeover dribble.

In the era of tight, man-to-man marking, only well-executed combination plays will carry the ball to an advanced position on the field. All players on a team must be capable of executing these combinations, and more importantly, be able to see where they belong in a game.

Chapter Five

Wall Passing

THE ESSENCE of modern soccer is in the ability of two players to combine and work together to advance the ball and get behind defenders. As a generalization, these relationships are collectively called *combinations*. They include takeovers, give-and-go's, overlaps and wall passes.

To teach any of these combinations the modern soccer coach must consider two basic factors:

1. A proper sequence of drills to be sure that the technical/tactical skill is learned.

2. The creation of situations that will allow players to know *when* to execute the skill.

The most basic of these skills is the *wall pass*, in which one player passes the ball to a teammate who one-touch passes the ball back into the path of the advancing first player. Thus, the first player acts as an aggressive attacking player, while the second remains passive and acts as a "wall" off which the first player plays and rebounds the ball.

In Diagram 5-1, player X_1 is the aggressive player, and X_2 is the passive wall. Assume that a defender is standing in the path of X_1, which forces him to execute the wall pass. Otherwise X_1 would proceed straight ahead without combining with X_2 for the wall pass.

The drills that follow demonstrate in sequence *how* to execute the

Diagram 5-1

wall pass. The drills end with game-like pressure. Your players will be lead to realize that the wall-pass situation is not so much found in a game as much as it is *created!*

Wall Passing with Eight Players

A grid of 40 yards to a side is marked with cones or corner flags at each of the four corners. A player with a ball is stationed at each corner. Then halfway down each side a player is stationed about 12 yards outside the grid.

1. In preparation to the drill work the eight players are arranged as seen in Diagram 5-2. On signal, each player with a ball dribbles in a clockwise direction. As he nears midpoint of a side, the waiting player moves in about 8 yards, takes the pass from the dribbler, and one-touch wall passes the ball back into the path of the dribbler. The dribbler runs around each side of the grid, wall passing with the outside player. In one complete rotation, the dribbler wall passes four times for technique and runs 160 yards for conditioning. See Diagram 5-3.

2. For inexperienced players, it is recommended that each player make two complete rotations around the grid. Then the wall player and the dribbler change places, and the drill is repeated. As a variation, the dribblers can run in a counter-clockwise direction.

3. The wall players can also be stationed inside the grid. The dribbler runs clockwise, as before, but passes to the right. Again, as the dribbler runs along the line, the wall player can run closer to the dribbler to help execute the wall pass.

This is a very important move that wall players must learn to make. The wall-pass situation is *created* by having a teammate appear

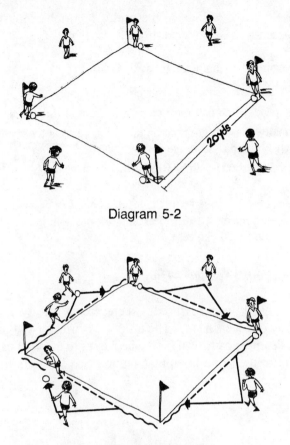

Diagram 5-2

Diagram 5-3

near a defender to support an advancing dribbler. The more sudden the movement the greater the chance of success. On the other hand, the closer that the wall passer is to the dribbler, the more demanding is the need for perfect technique and timing.

In effect, the wall passer signals that the wall pass is "on" when he moves to a supporting position to allow the wall pass to be executed. The marking defender is the final factor. If he drops off to mark the wall passer, the pass is "off." If the defender stays with the dribbler, then the wall pass is "on."

4. A final variation frees the wall player to stand outside or inside the grid. As each player dribbles around the corner, the "wall" can

station himself inside or outside the grid. The dribbler must look up and be prepared to pass either to his left or right.

Some points to watch for in wall passing:

- The wall player should one-touch pass the ball.
- The speed of the ball must carry it in front of the dribbler.
- Normally, the ball goes out on the second pass at the same angle on which it was passed to the wall.
- The wall passer should be 6 to 8 yards from the dribbler at the time of the pass.
- The ball can be passed with the inside of one foot or the outside of the other. Players must learn to explore all possibilities before making technical/tactical choices.

Wall Passing with Twelve Players

The same grid setup is used, except now a passive defender is added halfway down each side. The task of the dribbler is to dribble as close to the defender as he can before he passes to the wall passer. The drills are run in the same fashion as before. See Diagram 5-4.

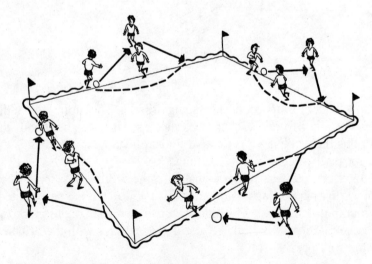

Diagram 5-4

1. The dribbler makes one full rotation of the grid wall passing four times. Then the players rotate positions.

2. The dribbler now moves in the reverse direction (counter-clockwise). The players rotate so that all have a turn at each position.

3. The wall passer can be stationed inside the grid, and the dribblers can run first clockwise and then counter-clockwise.

4. The defender can now apply pressure:

   a. The defender should move slowly at the dribbler. In this instance the defender begins from a starting position about 12 yards from the dribbler.

   b. The defender should move rapidly backward away from the dribbler, beginning about 4 yards from the corner marker.

   c. The defender is free to move either way ... backward or forward.

5. With the defender free to move backward or forward, the wall passer is free to station himself inside or outside the grid. It is essential that the wall passer stays even with the defender. The angle of passing is ruined if the wall player is not even with the defender. Also, in a game the wall may be left in an offside position.

The above drills can be run with a minimum of twelve players. Additional players can be added; they need only to wait for one rotation and then replace the dribbler or other active player in the drill while that player rests.

6. There are many variations that can be introduced into this basic routine. Some of the more popular ones are listed below. Others can be created according to local need.

   a. An "extra" player can be stationed at each corner of the grid. This will allow the dribbler to practice his ability to fake and turn at each corner.

   b. The wall player can move directly at the dribbler, instead of trying to stay even with the defender.

   c. The wall can square pass instead of lead passing the ball.

   d. The pace can move from slow to fast. (Make *sure* that the dribbler does not operate in one gear.)

   e. Finally, a second defender can be introduced to mark the wall. (This will be discussed shortly.)

The trainer has been given a checklist of things to look for in the performance of the wall player. Now he checks the dribbler for:

    a. Dribbling and passing techniques

    b. Pace—slow to fast

    c. Protecting the ball (this can be done at the corner where the extra man is standing)

    d. Feints—including to the defender

    e. Speed of dribbler following the first pass

    f. Speed of the ball—especially the first pass

    g. Willingness to go 1 v 1 with the defender (This must always be a final option for the dribbler to keep the defender on his toes.)

7. The role of the defender has been explained, but to review:

    a. He can move forward to the dribbler—slowly

    b. He can fall backward—rapidly

    c. He can hold his ground

    d. He can increase pressure to 100 percent

It is easy for the trainer to check on techniques when the drills are executed around the grid. This kind of organization allows the trainer to assume a central position where he can observe and supervise all the participants in a rather small area. As the level of technique increases, the size of the grid can be reduced to 30 yards a side, then 25, and finally 20 yards a side. The short distance will put high demands on the execution of the passes: speed, accuracy, timing. All of these variations will take time. Do not expect perfection in one or two practice sessions.

Wall Passing with Four Players

For an organized variation, the wall-passing drills can be run in a straight line. Instead of turning the corner of a grid and continuing, the drill is continued by reversing direction.

In a line 40 yards long, player A dribbles to defender B, passes to wall player D, runs around defender B, picks up the return wall pass, dribbles ahead and passes to player C who has been waiting. (See Diagram 5-5.) Now the drill is run in the opposite direction. The dribbler becomes the defender. (He should move back up to a midpoint.) The former defender goes to the opposite end. Now the drills looks like Figure 5-6.

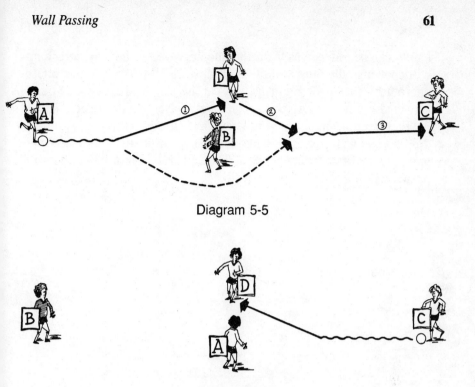

Diagram 5-5

Diagram 5-6

The three players in the line can continue to wall pass and reverse direction. After each fourth execution, the wall player should be replaced.

The variations of the grid can be introduced into this organization. Some to consider are:

1. Have the defender hold his position. Then allow him to move: first forward, then backward. Finally, free him to do as he wishes.

2. The wall player can first stand as a stationary target. Then he can move. First he moves closer to the defender, then he moves to the ball, (i.e., he moves to the dribbler). Finally, he moves to one side or the other of the path of the dribbler.

3. The defender can drop off to mark the wall player.

4. A second defender can be introduced. This will greatly change the complexion of the drills.

The line for the drill must be 40 yards long in the beginning. The length can be reduced as the technique improves. A line 20 yards long will challenge the most skillful of groups. The line organization offers one other advantage. Extra players can be stationed at each end and activated in rotation. Also, a second wall player can be added, so that the players move in rotation. In Diagram 5-7, the first player in line A dribbles and wall passes with player B. He picks up the return pass and passes to the first waiting player at line C. This player dribbles and wall passes with player D. And so forth.

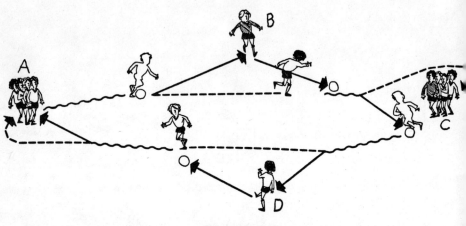

Diagram 5-7

Wall Passing on an Open Field

The final step in wall passing is on the open field. Many variations are available. A few are outlined below.

1. From midfield, a line of players can wall pass left and right with a finish on goal. Players X_1 and X_2 stand as stationary wall players. At first the shot is taken to an open goal. Then a goalkeeper can be added. See Diagram 5-8.

2. Two lines can be set up at midfield. The players can wall pass, finish with a shot on goal, and get on the end of the other line.

In Diagram 5-9 the player in line #1 wall passes, finishes with a shot, and, instead of getting to the end of line #2, the player becomes the wall player for the second line. Then he can move to the end of that

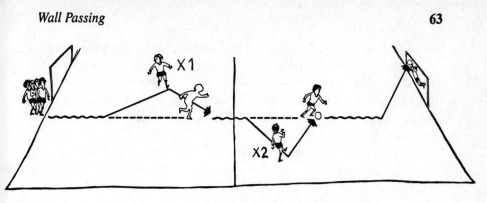

Diagram 5-8

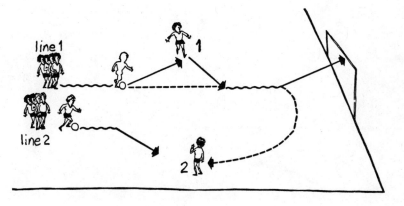

Diagram 5-9

line. The wall player in position #2 should *move* in the direction of the dribbler coming from line #2.

This makes the drill for players on line #2 much more difficult. The player dribbling from line #2 must wall pass with a moving teammate. This means that in rotation, the player wall passes with a stationary wall and then with a moving wall. The moving wall will challenge the timing and pacing of the players. The moving wall can move left or right of the dribbler, as well as come forward from the goal line.

3. A defender can be introduced to mark the dribbler. The pressure by the defender can be slight at first and finally increased to 100 percent. When the defender is giving a full effort, the dribbler can try to carry the ball behind the defender without wall passing. This final variation must be controlled by the trainer.

The wall-passing drills can end by having the defender move to mark the wall player instead of the dribbler. If the dribbler is instructed to pass, marked or not, the wall player will have pressure put on him by the defender. If the defender positions himself behind and to the side, he can effectively prevent the wall pass from being completed. See Diagram 5-10.

However, this does not prevent the two attackers from still working together. The wall player can either back pass or square pass the ball to the dribbler. Strictly speaking, this combination is no longer a wall pass, but is now a combination that is called *give-and-go*. This is a separate subject that will be covered in the next section.

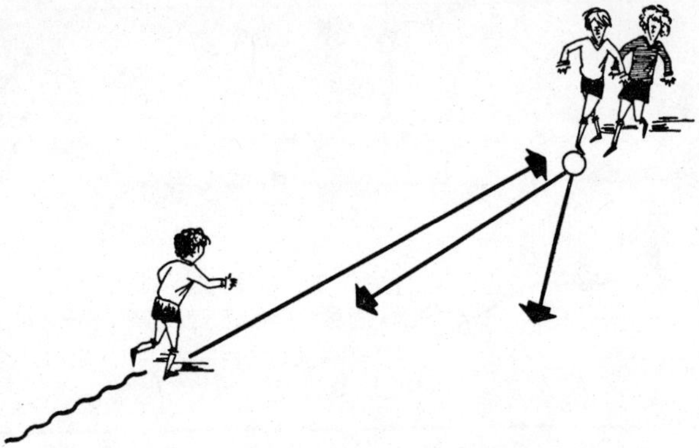

Diagram 5-10

Chapter Six

The Give-and-Go Combination

In ADDITION TO THE wall-pass combination, two teammates can learn to work together by using the give-and-go.

What is meant by the "give-and-go"? How is it executed? How can it be recognized by the players? These are some of the questions that we shall now consider. This combination is as basic as the wall pass and must be learned to be executed with equal skill as the wall pass. Consider the situation in Diagram 6-1.

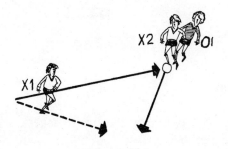

Diagram 6-1

Player X_1 dribbles downfield and passes to X_2, who is being marked by defender O_1. As soon as X_1 passes the ball to X_2 he runs to the left or right to receive a return pass. X_1 has run to the right for the return pass. It must be noted from the beginning of this section that the first player in these drills, X_1, signals for a return pass by running rapidly to the left or right. He does not call for the ball by yelling. His sudden movement is the call for the ball. This is part of the Dutch system of *silent calling* for the ball. It is also part of the *pacing system*, where a slow run is followed by sudden, rapid sprinting. This was explained in Chapter Four, "The Dutch System."

The movement of the drill continues. After player X_1 receives the return pass from X_2, player X_2 turns *away* from X_1, and runs downfield (Figure 6-2). The defender will be watching the ball go to X_1, so that X_2 is turning on the defender's "blind" side. Then player X_1 passes to X_2. This final pass is called a "through" pass. This combination of passes and running is the basic demonstration of the give-and-go.

The give-and-go combination can be learned in two-man and three-man drills. After the players learn how to execute the combination, they must learn *when* it can be used in a game. Five aside scrimmages and six-on-four scrimmages will provide opportunities for this.

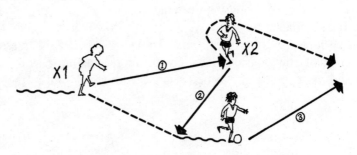

Diagram 6-2

Two-man drills

The basic drill is run by the two attackers, with the defender omitted. In Diagram 6-3, player X_1 dribbles toward X_2 who is waiting upfield. Remember that player X_2 is not *standing* and waiting. He is running against an imaginary defender, and then turning to face his teammate and receive the first pass. This movement is called "checking in and checking out." That is, check in by going against the defender ... push him back and make space; check out by turning and receiving the ball in the created space.

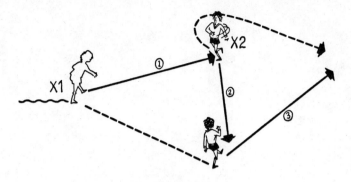

Diagram 6-3

Player X_2 traps the ball. Meantime, X_1 has run *rapidly* to the right, signaling that he wants the ball. By the time the ball is passed, X_1 has advanced enough to receive a square pass. Player X_2 turns to the right, the blind side, and receives a through pass from X_1.

The sequence:

1. Push pass from X_1 to X_2
2. Square pass from X_2 to X_1
3. Through pass from X_1 to X_2

Now the players turn and run the drill in the opposite direction. (See Diagram 6-4.)

This basic sequence should be practiced until the players understand and can execute this technique. When the drill is going well, player X_2 can one-touch the ball to his teammate.

Some variations:

1. Begin with a soft pass, then make it harder.
2. Each player traps and then passes.
3. Player X_2 one-touches the ball.
4. Both players one-touch the ball.
5. Increase the distance between the players for the first pass.
6. Increase the distance of the through pass.
7. Put the ball in the air.
8. Add a defender. Increase pressure from 50 percent to 100 percent.

The role of X_2 can be changed as he becomes familiar with the

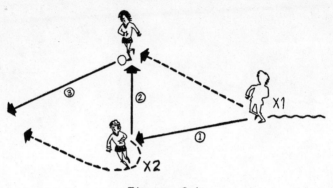

Diagram 6-4

drill. In the beginning he is concerned with back passing, turning and running for a pass. He can be instructed to *turn with the ball*. Again, he should turn to the defender's blind side and square pass to his open teammate. Then he can use the various turns and feints that he learned in Chapter One, "Dribbling—Turning—Feinting." These turns should be reviewed and introduced one at a time. The initial opposition should be passive.

The turning of X_2 with the ball is more time-consuming than one-touch passing. If player X_1 runs at a normal pace he will be beyond the point of receiving a square pass. This may result in X_2 delivering a *through* pass to X_1. Obviously, there can be no further combinations given, as this through pass should carry the ball and teammate well upfield.

As player X_2 turns more quickly with the ball, then the second pass can be the regular square pass followed by the through pass back to X_2. Good soccer players must have *quick* feet. Turning the ball is an example of when quickness is more important than *speed*. Timing is another element players must learn in order to anticipate each other's speed of running and quickness in turning, so that there is little time or space given for an opponent to win the ball.

From Midfield

Form a line at midfield. The first player moves out to check in/ check out. The second player trails behind and then begins the pass sequence push-pass, square pass, through pass. The drill ends with the first player taking a shot on goal, and the second player takes his place.

Then the various turns and feints can be added to the drill. Finally, a marking defender can be added (perhaps a player who finished the drill). See Diagram 6-5.

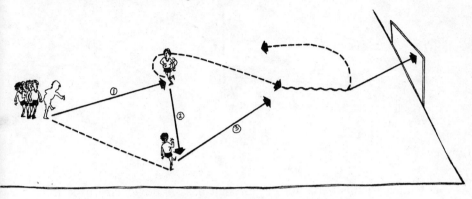

Diagram 6-5

Three Players

The basic drill can be run with three players who rotate positions as the drill is reversed. See Diagram 6-6. When the sequence of rotation and reversing direction is running smoothly, the variations mentioned previously can be introduced. Diagram 6-7 shows yet another variation in which three players run the drill without a

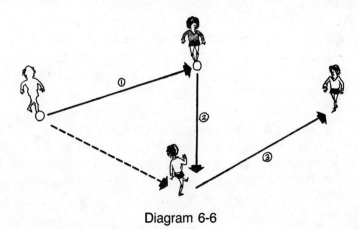

Diagram 6-6

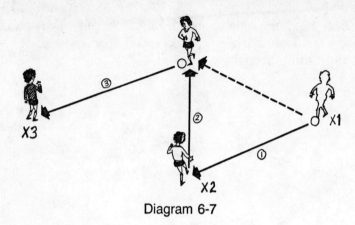

Diagram 6-7

defender. In this variation the through pass is delivered to the third player. Then the same exercise is run in the opposite direction.

Three Players in an Open Area

After this variation (Diagram 6-7) has been learned, there is yet another one that has the middle man in a fixed position. This is an excellent drill for teaching a selected player ball control with turns and feints.

Player X_1 passes to X_2. Then X_1 makes his quick move to signal the return pass. This is followed by a through pass to X_3. Player X_3 passes to X_2 and runs to signal the return pass. Meantime, X_1 has run back to his starting point to receive the through pass from X_3, as shown in Diagram 6-8.

This drill can begin as a two-touch exercise until the players understand the sequence. Then variations can be introduced.

1. The center player can make a half-turn to pass directly to X_3. This is called a 1-2-3 combination. Begin with X_1 push passing to X_2 and then on to X_3.

2. From a pass by X_1, the center player can make a three-quarter turn to pass back to X_1 in his new position (Diagram 6-9). This is called a 1-2-1 combination. At first, the combination must be controlled by the trainer. Later, the players are free to exercise any combination that they want.

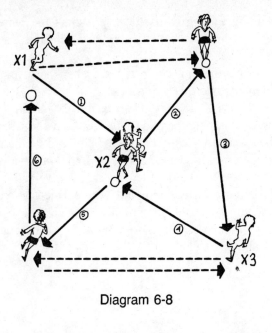

Diagram 6-8

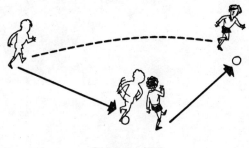

Diagram 6-9

To review one vital point: The key to the execution of the give-and-go combination is the movement of the player *without* the ball; he controls the pass; he controls the pace; he controls the timing. In continental soccer, the players on the field control the action of the player with the ball. Unselfish running and unselfish passing are the keys to teamwork. *Teamwork is the key to success.*

This point cannot be too strongly emphasized. Game control is obtained by movement off the ball, when your team has ball possession. Loud calling for the ball will only distract the player with the ball. Also, loud calling will call attention to a defender that a player is open.

Movement off the ball controls the game; the give-and-go drill will clearly demonstrate this point.

After these variations have been practiced, a scrimmage of five aside or six aside will help the players to see when and where the give-and-go can be executed. Restrictions can be placed on the scrimmage; goals can be scored only from the give-and-go combination.

If the players are struggling to execute the give-and-go combination, one player on each team should be identified as an unmarked sweeper or "schemer." Being unmarked, he can easily execute the first pass of the combination. A more spontaneous execution of the combination should follow after a few restricted scrimmages.

Chapter Seven

Three-Man Combinations

IN THE PREVIOUS SECTION, "Give-and-Go Combinations," one drill variation introduced a third attacking player with 1-2-1 and 1-2-3 combinations. Such combinations should serve as an introduction for true three-man passing combinations. But the real work is yet to come.

Three-man passing combinations are the keystone to modern soccer. By execution, there is always a long pass which opens up the game. Also, there is back passing which gives width to the attack and creates "blind-side" runs away from the ball. Within the three-man combinations there can be found the two-man combinations—wall passing, give-and-go, etc. The variations and creativeness are limited only by the ability of the players themselves.

The Basic Drill

In an area about 20 yards by 20 yards, three players are stationed, one in the center and the other two in adjacent corners. One corner player passes to the middle man and runs to the nearest open center. The middle man back passes to the third player, who delivers the ball to the diagonally opposite corner where the first player has run.

In Diagram 7-1 the three passes are seen as follows: Player X_1 passes to X_2 and begins his run. Player X_2 back passes to X_3, who starts running out of his corner slowly. Then X_3 delivers the long pass to X_1,

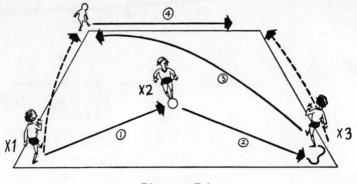

Diagram 7-1

in the diagonally opposite corner. Finally X₃ runs to his adjacent corner and receives a square pass back from X₁. Now the drill can be run in the opposite direction. X₃ passes to X₂, who back passes to X₁, who delivers the long pass to X₃. After a short square pass from X₃ to X₁, the drill is ready to be run again.

This drill should be familiar to many coaches; it is often called "up-back-and-through." However, it is really not just another drill but a keystone to the almost infinite variations of combinations that are available to groups of three players.

Finishing

Before we examine some of the three-man combinations, let's say a few words about *finishing*. Consider the options of the right outside attacker as he penetrates with the ball through the final third of the field. As he moves to the edge of the penalty area and enters the 18-yard box, he has many options:

1. He can drive directly at the near post for a shot on goal.
2. If opposed, he can square pass to his left to a teammate in a more centered position.
3. He can cross the ball to the opposite side to a teammate approaching on the defender's blind side, beyond the far post.
4. He can carry the ball to the goal line, somewhere between the 6-yard spot and the edge of the penalty box. From this position he can execute an angled back pass to one or more players attacking from the central positions.

Of the four options, the last is the most versatile. The advantages are many:

  a. No player is offside on this pass.
  b. The ball is moving *away* from the goalkeeper.
  c. The ball is moved into a more central and dangerous position.

In the drills that follow, the options that were just listed must be assumed as being available to the attacking player even when all such options are not placed in a given diagram or drill. To review, an outside attacker can:

  1. Attack the goal directly
  2. Square in the ball on a pass
  3. Cross the ball to a defender's blind side
  4. Carry to the end line for a back, angle pass

These are the finish electives that are available to the player with the ball. With these electives in mind, let's return to three-man combinations.

First Option

The first option is simply placing the basic pattern on a half field.

In Diagram 7-2, the drill begins with X_1 passing "up" to X_2. Then X_2 back passes to X_3, who delivers the long through pass to X_1. He then square passes out to X_3, who carries the ball toward the goal line and centers the ball, shoots or executes any of the four options mentioned before.

A simple variation of this drill is shown in Diagram 7-3, in which the play begins with an "up" pass by X_3.

Then X_2 back passes to X_1 who through passes to X_3 advancing along the touchline. Player X_3 has the same finishing electives as above. The initial pass can come from an inside or outside player; the finish is the same; the variations are the same. Initially, the through pass should be delivered on the ground, but as the players acquire skill in passing and receiving, the through pass can be delivered through the air. Then any of the passes can be given in the air.

Once the variations are running well, defenders can be intro-

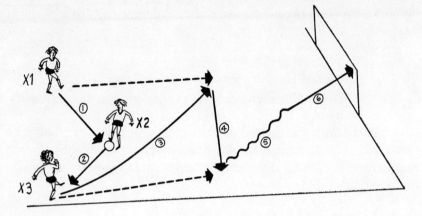

Diagram 7-2

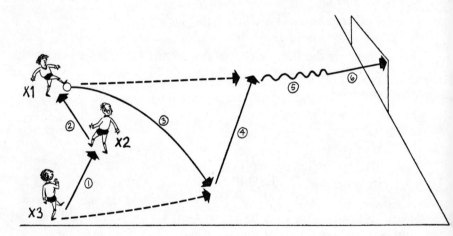

Diagram 7-3

duced. First a defender can mark the middle player, so that he can check in/check out in a game-like way. Then a second defender can be placed in front of the goal. As the outside player advances with the ball, the drill becomes 3 on 1 plus a keeper. This makes the final pass by the outside player more difficult. In addition to facing the defensive players, the attackers have the additional problem of becoming *predictable*. To reduce predictability, introduce additional variations.

Second Option

Several variations can be used by having the outside player check in/check out. Now the first pass is delivered by the middle player of the group of three.

In Diagram 7-4, player X_2 begins the drill by passing to the outside of X_3. Player X_3 square passes to X_1, who has been running straight ahead. Player X_1 now delivers a through pass to X_3, who turns blind side of the defender and runs on to the delivered ball. Now X_3 has the usual finishing options:

1. Shot on goal
2. Square pass inside
3. Cross beyond far post
4. Dribble to end line

As a variation of this drill, player X_2 can run an overlap of X_3 when he has made the first pass. Player X_2 must run for the goal following his square pass. Player X_2 receives the through pass from X_1 and makes the finishing pass/run options.

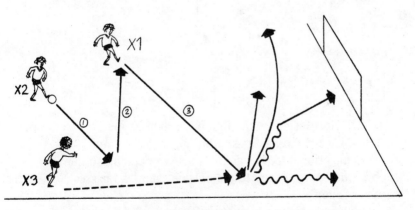

Diagram 7-4

Initially, defenders can be stationed as they were earlier: marking the advanced player, X_3, and zone-defending the goalmouth. The amount of freedom that the defenders are given is relative to the ability of the attackers. The drill must be allowed to succeed; opposition must stiffen when they succeed easily. At first, we instruct the defenders to mark the man, and not go for the ball. When the drill runs very well, a third defender can be introduced. Another possibility would be for the initial organization to have two marking defenders and a final "free" man, or last man.

There are several options that X_3 can try when the ball is passed to him. Instead of square passing inside, X_3 can dribble inside. As he dribbles squarely across the field, X_3 should turn suddenly and deliver a long, lead pass to his teammate running down the touchline. Which teammate is running down the touchline?

If X_2 begins an overlap when he passes to X_3, then the pass is obviously to X_2 running in the overlapping position. See Diagram 7-5.

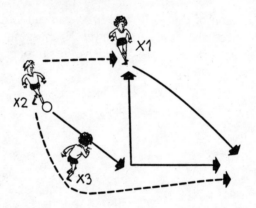

Diagram 7-5

If X_2 runs inside on the first pass, then X_1 must make the run to the touchline for the lead pass from X_3. See Diagram 7-6.

On the dribble-in, X_3 can run a takeover combination with X_1 who dribbles the opposite way to the outside, and lead passes X_2 who has run the overlap.

Who determines which variation to use? As can be seen in the variations just presented, the movement of the player making the first pass, *after the pass*, is the movement that controls the drill. As we stated from the very beginning of this handbook, the movement of the player *with* the ball is controlled by players *without* the ball.

The importance of the role of the player without the ball cannot be

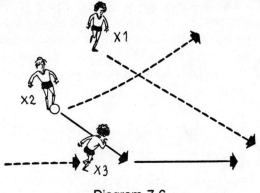

Diagram 7-6

too strongly stressed. Players must learn to *move* after they pass the ball. They may move in the same direction as the ball to offer support. They may run to a more advanced position, or they may run an overlap. But standing and watching is what spectators do, not what ballplayers do.

Additional Variations

There are a few more variations that can be covered. The center player X_2 can square pass the ball to the outside. This will require X_3 to run on to the ball. See Diagram 7-7.

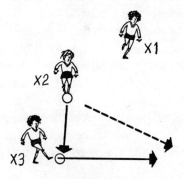

Diagram 7-7

While this is happening, X_2 runs on an angle to the touchline and receives a pass downfield from X_3. Now the two players switch positions. With X_2 in a forward position on the touchline, player X_3 runs for the near post. As a variation, three players can approach an advanced player and run the same drill. Now the advanced player runs to the touchline, and X_3, who is farthest from the goal, stays behind to act as the advanced player for the next group. See Diagram 7-8.

Diagram 7-8

Player X_1 passes up to the advanced player who square passes the ball to X_3. Then the advanced player turns on the blind side of the defender and runs to the touchline for the return pass from X_3. Then X_3 waits for the next group to advance. When the advanced player moves after his pass, he must then learn to turn on the blind side of the defender—the side away from the ball—and make his run.

Defenders must learn to watch their opponents. Ball watching is a dangerous habit. Attackers can "get free" easily by turning away from the ball or blind side of the defender. As attackers learn to make the blind side turn an automatic move, the effectiveness of the defenders will be reduced to a minimum.

If the ball is square passed inside, then the advanced player runs for the far post and X_3 runs down the touchline for the through pass from X_1. Now X_2 replaces the advanced player, and the drill ends in the usual way.

Also, if the middle player square passes or back passes to the same side from which he received the ball, that is normally a signal that a wall pass will follow. This is seen in Diagram 7-9.

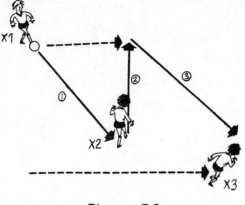

Diagram 7-9

Player X₁ passes up to X₂ who square passes back to X₁. Now X₂ runs ahead to a support position to execute the wall pass with X₁, who then passes to X₃ running down the sideline.

If too much attention is called to the progress of the ball down one side of the field, the defensive unit can be surprised by having the ball delivered to the opposite side to an overlapping fullback.

Player X₂ can square pass to the left of the fullback, or player X₁ can do this following the wall-pass combination. Since the fullback creates a fourth attacking position, and we are now concentrating on the three-man units, we will not dwell on the possibilities. It is sufficient to say that overlapping fullbacks add yet another dimension to the game. However, fullbacks will not run up on the attack unless the ball is *delivered* to them. There must be a payoff for the defender who has run the overlap.

Twin Strikers

One final variation will demonstrate how the up-back-through concept works with *two* advanced players.

In Diagram 7-10, player X₃ passes to X₁ who square passes to X₂, the other striker. Then X₂ back passes to X₃ who has moved straight forward. After X₁ and X₂ have passed the ball, they each run a criss-cross pattern that carries them to the opposite goal post. This gives X₃ some options, but let us look at what happens on the crisscross runs.

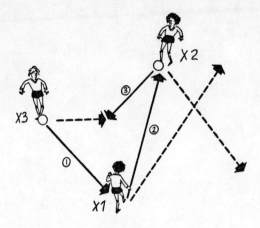

Diagram 7-10

If X_1 square passes and runs toward the left post, X_2 may be able to deliver a lead pass to X_1 knowing where his run will carry him. Or, X_3 can one-touch the ball in the same direction to X_1. Then X_1 can square out to X_2 who is now on the right. Then X_2 can shoot or carry the ball to the goal line as with all previous drill options.

If there is good defensive pressure, player X_3 can pass to X_2 running to the outside right.

If defenders are marking X_1 and X_2, and they follow these two in crisscross, there is nothing to stop X_3 from running in for a direct shot on goal. If a defender drops off his marked attacker at the last minute, then the wall pass is "on," as the defender has created a 2 v 1 situation.

Players must learn to read these variations as they appear on the field. Reducing the attack 2 v 1 in front of the goal gives the numerical superiority to the attackers. They must use the opportunity for the brief time that they enjoy having it.

Suppose that X_3 began by passing to X_2 on the first pass? There are many possible variations—think about it!

Review

You have seen the three-man combinations begin with up-back-through passes. Then familiar combinations were added: wall passes, takeover from a dribble, overlapping, place changing, and crosses to the opposite side. The variations are almost limitless, but certain patterns begin to emerge.

1. The finish (shot on goal) electives are always the same.
2. Movement following a pass has a direct effect on the combination that develops.
3. Participants can quickly learn and recognize the various patterns.
4. Variations are available to reduce predictability.

In summary, three-man passing combinations are the keystone of modern soccer; they can absorb all two-man combinations to present an almost infinite variety of attack patterns to defenders.

Modern soccer cannot exist without three-man combinations.

Chapter Eight

Combination Finishing Drill

THIS DRILL IS nothing more than a continuation of the first section on dribbling and feinting. The players are placed on the field and end the drill with a shot on goal. The Dutch call this, "Dribbling from a given pass over the left or right wing, finishing with a shot on goal." (See Diagram 8-1.)

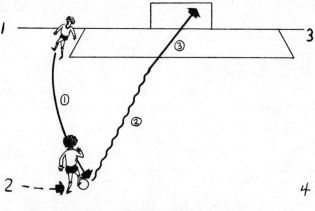

Diagram 8-1

The players are divided into four groups and evenly stationed in the four corners of the half field. The same drill is run alternately on each side of the field. If only a few players are available, then the drill is run on only one side of the field.

One player from midfield area #2 (or #4), steps forward and calls for the ball to be passed from the near corner. This calling is done silently by the sudden movement of the player. He can also point to the direction in which the ball is to be passed.

This player then runs to the passed ball, controls it, dribbles to the edge of the penalty area, and shoots. Then the dribbler goes to the corner (area #1) and the passer goes to midfield (area #2). Now the drill is run using stations #3 and #4.

When this drill is running smoothly, variations can be introduced.

Pass Variations

The first variations are related to the pass:

1. Begin by passing on the ground to the near side.
2. Then the ball can be passed in the air to the near side. (If the distance is too great for the players, the coach should move the players in area #1 along the touchline closer to midfield.)
3. Finally, the ball can be crossed from corner #1 to the opposite midfield area #4.

Dribbling Variations

1. After the player in area #1 passes the ball, he runs up to the touchline and acts as a "wall." Then the dribbler wall passes with him and finishes with the shot on goal.
2. A defender can be stationed in the penalty area. Now the dribbler wall passes, beats the defender with a feint, and shoots on goal.
3. A sweeper can be added behind the marking defender. In this situation, the marking defender must be instructed to give only 50 percent effort, so that the dribbler can reach the sweeper. (After all, this is a drill for attackers, not defenders!)
4. A series of poles can be placed on the field forcing the dribbler to slalom to the goal. (The wall pass is eliminated for this variation.)
5. The regular goal can be replaced by one or two smaller goals to make the finishing shot more difficult. Two corner flags can be used to make the goal shooting area small; corner areas can be marked as the targets.

6. Finally, the goalkeeper can be stationed behind the goal. From this position, at the last moment, he can signal to the dribbler and indicate to which corner of the goal the ball should be shot. Of course, this situation will force the dribbler to look up as he nears the goal. This kind of drill is popular in Holland, and is used near the end of a practice session before a scrimmage.

The variations presented here are but a few that may be used from the same general *organization*. The actual drills must reflect the needs of a given team as perceived by the coach.

As an example, weak shooting teams will not face defenders in the penalty area. Strong teams will face a sweeper in addition to marking defenders.

These decisions are up to the individual coach.

Section III

Numerical Superiority

So far we have covered two major aspects of training: the development of individual technique, and the association of two or more players in the coordination of technique in what is called combination play.

The initial emphasis was on technique, and by increasing the size of the drill area, we introduced a *conditioning* element on the training. Increasing the *size* of the circle increased the emphasis on conditioning. Also, we increased the number of repetitions for the same purpose. Running the wall pass twice around a 40-yard grid is an example of this kind of conditioning work.

At the very lowest level we also introduced some *tactical* concepts. Any time a player has a choice where to move to or where to pass the ball, such choices are considered to be *tactical*.

Now we are ready to place emphasis on the tactical aspects of the game. While player choice is tactical, the heart or core of soccer tactics is in creating *numerical superiority near the ball*, and using this superiority to advantage: advance the ball up the field and score goals. All team formations and systems of play are reduced to this singular and simple tactic—create numerical superiority near the ball.

Throughout a soccer game, as the ball is moved from area to area, situations are created where numerical superiority is gained and lost. Sometimes the numerical superiority is lost because the ball is lost due to poor technique. More often the advantage is lost because the players either fail to recognize the numerical superiority when it is achieved, or they do not know how to use such superiority for their own advantage.

The purpose of this section is to train groups of players to recognize and use numerical superiority.

There are limits to recognizing numerical superiority. Players can neither see nor use such an advantage in an 11 v 10 situation. Rather, let us approach the problem from the opposite direction; the limits will then become more obvious.

1. *Two-against-one.* Any advantage situation on the field is reduced to this—two players with the ball attacking a sole defender. If the defender is "played out," the ball can be advanced with an unmarked attacker. The goal of any numerical superiority situation is to reduce it to 2 : 1 and then to play out the defender.

2. *Three-against-one.* This ratio creates a two-man difference between the attackers and defenders. Such a ratio creates situations that makes it very easy for the attackers to recognize the numerical superiority when it occurs on the field. In many ways this is the basic ratio for training players. It is a ratio that can be sustained long enough for drill purposes; the 2 : 1 ratio is too fatiguing to sustain over any reasonable period of time.

3. *Three-against-two.* Any time numerical superiority is achieved on the field, it is subject to change. The greatest source of change is the addition of a new defender. *Delay* is a basic principle of defense, and time will produce more defenders. Players in the 3 : 1 situation must be prepared to see that situation erode rapidly to 3 : 2.

4. *Four-against-two*. Here again the ratio gives a two-player difference between the attackers and defenders. This situation differs from the last three examples because the emphasis is placed on the long pass. (This will be explained later.) The emphasis on the long pass is basic to the continental game of soccer.

5. *Four-against-three*. Greater pressure is placed on the attackers as they search out the single unmarked teammate. In many ways this is a final or ultimate drill ratio used to teach numerical superiority. Pace, ball possession, support and a deep man are all elements of this drill.

Higher ratio drills are variations of the basic drill ratios listed above. Six-on-four drills reduce to three-on-two; eight-on-six ratios reduce to four-on-three. Thus, this section will end with a maximum of four on one side.

Chapter Nine

Two Attackers

THE TWO AGAINST ONE combination in an open area can be thought of as a simple game of "keep away," with the object being to have X_2 keep the ball away from the defender O_1. (Diagram 9-1.) Normally, the player with the ball has the easiest position in the drill. The defender must race from one player to another in a vain attempt to just touch the ball.

Diagram 9-1

If he just touches the ball he then replaces the passer. After one minute he is also replaced. The player supporting the man with the ball also has a difficult task. He must make wide runs in an arc, to get from the dead space behind the defender. (See Diagram 9-2.) A few short steps to the side by the defender will force the support player either to run yet wider on the arc, or to reverse direction and run in a wide arc in the opposite direction.

Diagram 9-2

In a short time all the players are tired, but most of the work has been done *without* the ball.

There are a series of drills that will develop team skills and polish combinations that can be put directly into the game.

1. *The hard pass.* Assume that the players begin as in Diagram 9-2, with the support player having successfully run to the side in an arc. (See Diagram 9-3A.) The player with the ball, X_1, has his

Diagram 9-3A

teammate in sight and can deliver a hard pass to that player's feet. The pass should be hard to get beyond the reach of the defender. Thus the first combination is a hard pass to a teammate's feet. See Diagram 9-3B.

Diagram 9-3B

2. *The soft pass*. There will be occasions when the support player cannot get from behind the defender. Then the pass must be played into space. This pass must be a soft pass. It must be soft for two reasons. To begin with, since the support player must run onto the ball, it is more difficult to control. Timing becomes critical. With the defender changing direction, the player wants to control the pass as quickly as possible. The soft pass helps to establish this control.

The second reason is that as the support player reaches the ball he should have eye contact with his teammate. He wants to see where his teammate is running after the pass, and he wants to keep his teammate in sight in the event that he needs to pass quickly back to him. (See Diagram 9-4.)

Diagram 9-4

If a hard pass is delivered beyond the support player, he must turn, with his back to the passer, and chase the ball to bring it under control. It is an easy task for the defender to get between these two players and isolate the man with the ball.

Now both of these variations can be practiced at once: a hard pass to feet, and a soft pass to space.

3. *The through pass.* There are occasions when the two attacking players are side by side as they approach the defender. Then the man with the ball can make a lead pass between the defender and the support player. This is called a "through" pass, since the ball is passed through the space between the defender and support player. (See Diagram 9-5.) Again, this pass must be delivered so that eye contact is maintained. A hard pass downfield is wrong, as explained in combination #2 above.

Diagram 9-5

4. *Go alone.* In Diagram 9-5, the player with the ball dribbled to the defender and then made the through pass to his teammate. Some defenders, sensing that the pass is about to be delivered, will drop to an area between the two advancing players to prevent the pass. (See Diagram 9-6.)

Diagram 9-6

In such a situation, the player with the ball should be instructed to carry the ball beyond the defender and continue downfield with his teammate continuing to run nearby for support. This can be called "going alone" or "burning" the defender. After the players have learned all the combinations, then and only then, should they be allowed the "go alone" option. Otherwise, combination drills are abandoned for the chance to go one-on-one with the defender. This point must be stressed.

5. *The wall pass*. There will be times when the support player can get into a position beside the defender, after having been behind the defender. This offers the opportunity to execute a wall pass as shown in Diagrams 9-7A and 9-7B. The wall pass should be a one-touch pass as

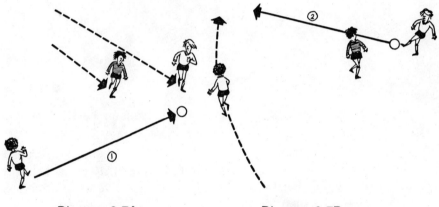

Diagram 9-7A   Diagram 9-7B

described in the section on wall passing. After this combination is executed smoothly, the player with the ball can be offered the choice of initiating the wall pass or "going alone."

6. *Outside takeover*. In an open space there will be occasions when the player with the ball can carry the ball to his teammate by dribbling. It is best that the dribbler uses his body to screen the ball from the defender, as he moved toward his support player.

In Diagram 9-8 the dribbler is seen carrying the ball with the inside of his right foot, so that the ball is opposite the side of the defender. As the two players approach each other, the support player will take over the control of the ball with the same foot as the dribbler,

Diagram 9-8

so that the ball is suddenly carried in the opposite direction. (See Diagrams 9-9A and 9-9B.)

Diagram 9-9A   Diagram 9-9B

At the last second the dribbler has only to withdraw his foot and the support player can assume control of the ball. Remember that a right foot dribble is taken over by the right foot; a left foot dribble is taken over by the left foot.

After the takeover is mastered, the dribbler can be given the option to keep the ball and just let the support player run by without receiving the ball. During a game, the task of the defender is made more difficult if the takeover combination is executed and then later on it is faked. This is another "go alone" variation.

7. *Inside takeover.* In the situation described before, the defender, sensing that he might be tricked, may back away from the dribbler to be more prepared to pick up another player. This creates space between the dribbler and the defender so that the ball can be taken over on the *inside* rather than the outside. (See Diagram 9-10.)

Notice that again the same foot is used on the takeover. In Diagram 9-10 the ball was carried on the left foot, and picked up on the takeover by the left foot. Actually, there is an advantage in this

Diagram 9-10

takeover, since the support player takes over the ball with his outside foot. This gives the ball automatic screening from the defender.

Again, when this combination is mastered, the dribbler has the option to keep the ball and "go alone." To review, the two-against-one combinations are as follows:

a. Hard pass to feet   e. Outside takeover

b. Soft pass to space   f. Inside takeover

c. Through pass   g. "Go alone"

d. Wall pass

When the above combinations have been mastered, practice may be conducted in the following organization.

1. *Six players—two goals.* The format is simple. Three teams of two are placed in a marked area with a goal at each end. One team of two players attacks a goal defended by one player and a goalkeeper. When a goal is scored or the ball is won, the defenders carry the ball to the opposite goal and try to score. The former attackers become the defenders. There is a perpetual motion of one team attacking, one defending and one resting at the opposite end of the field. See Diagram 9-11.

Diagram 9-11

This could be considered a form of interval training. Also, with each attack, the teams can be instructed how to attack ... i.e., wall pass, outside takeover, etc. Finally, they can be allowed to exercise any option that they want.

2. *Five players*. In a small area players Y_1 and Y_2 try to carry the ball beyond X_1 to player X_2, who is stationary and acting as a goal. If X_2 or X_1 touches the ball, it is considered to be a goal. (See Diagram 9-12.) Then X_1 or X_2 passes the ball back to Y_1 or Y_2 who attacks in the opposite direction. When play gets to be smooth, the stationary end men one-touch pass the ball back into play. The defenders should be replaced every minute and the attackers every three minutes.

Diagram 9-12

3. *Four players—two goals*. Here, a team of two players attacks one defender and a goalkeeper. When the ball is turned over, the defenders attack the opposite goal, which the former attackers defend with one field defender and one goalkeeper. (See Diagram 9-13.)

4. *Four players*. Two teams of two players each are placed in a grid, 20 yards by 20 yards. Several games can be played in this organization:

    a. Remaining players surround the grid and watch to critique the work of the players in the grid. The participants play 2 : 1 with the extra player waiting on the side. Each time the defender *touches* the ball, he is replaced by the waiting player. After a stated time, the play of attackers is critiqued and four more players are rotated into the grid.

Diagram 9-13

b. As soon as the defender wins the ball, the resting player joins him. The player who lost the ball moves off the grid to become the new resting player.

c. When the defender wins the ball, he begins to work with the supporting attacker. The attacker who lost the ball leaves the grid, and the resting player becomes the defender.

5. *Eight players*. Two teams of two can play while the rest wait. They can rotate positions every two or three minutes. Again, the attackers can be instructed on what combination to use, wall pass, takeover, etc., and then are allowed to use any option.

6. *With keepers*. If the players are available, goalkeepers can be added to defend each goal. The play remains the same.

7. *Half-field with team*. A final drill involves the whole team on half a field. Groups of two form at midfield. A goalkeeper is placed in the goalmouth, with a single defender stationed in front of him. The remaining players are placed in a corner, as in Diagram 9-14. On signal, player X_2 passes the ball to two-player team X_8 waiting in the center circle. They attack the goal, using a combination pass, carry the ball beyond X_1 and shoot on goal. Then a rotation is made. The member of X_8 who took the shot replaces X_1. Both X_1 and X_2 move to the end of the midfield line. The remaining member of the X_8 group gets on line behind X_7. Now X_3 passes to team X_9 at center circle, and the drill continues.

"On signal" means that the signal is to be given by a player waiting at the center circle. The player raises his arm as a "silent" signal that the ball is to be passed to him. Or he can point left or right—where the ball is to be played into space. (Remember, hard to feet and soft to space!)

Diagram 9-14

When this drill is running smoothly, a sweeper can be added behind the marking defender. The sweeper would not participate in the rotation. Other variations can be introduced according to need.

To review: This is a simple exercise that involves only three players. Each has a specific task to perform. The coach should review the tasks of each player:

1. *The attacker with the ball.* If he carries the ball directly *at the defender,* the supporting attacker is free of a marking defender.
2. *The support player.* He must stay *open* for a pass from the ball carrier. Sudden, rapid movement is the signal for a pass.
3. *Combinations.* The two attackers have many combinations available, such as the wall pass, the through pass, an outside dribbling takeover, an inside dribbling takeover, the overlap (follow the pass and run by your teammate) and a forward pass (when your teammate makes a deep run behind the defender).
4. *The defender.* The defender has two major roles. He must *position* himself so that the ball carrier cannot pass to his teammate. Having

done that, the defender must *press* for the ball—hunt the attacker with the ball—smother him—shut him down!

The 2:1 drill will quickly wear out the best of players. If the participants are frequently rotated, the various drills will work. Otherwise, the drill will have to end shortly.

It is best if you consider these drills to be *demonstration* drills. In all the drills that follow, it is possible to reduce the ratio to 2 : 1 and "play out" the defender, probably by the wall pass.

A few additional words about the wall pass are appropriate at this point.

1. The wall pass can be executed at almost any place on the field. When it is done on the top of the box (the 18-yard-line), it should be followed by a strong, serious threat to the goalkeeper. However, when done further downfield, it may be followed by a long pass upfield. A drill to practice this can be constructed with four players. As in a former wall-pass drill, player X_1 passes to X_2, who wall passes back to him. (See Diagram 9-15.) However, now X_1 delivers a *long* pass to X_3 more than 20-30 yards away. Then X_1 becomes the defender, and the drill is run in the opposite direction.

Diagram 9-15

2. The wall-pass variation must be practiced well enough that it can be delivered in the presence of a *second* defender. There are several variations that can be practiced. Let us first consider the basic alignment of players. The presence of the second defender presents the following problem:

Player X_1 dribbles forward at defender O_1 (Diagram 9-16). Teammate X_2 moves in to help by being available for a wall pass, but is closely marked. What to do?

Diagram 9-16

a. With practice, the one-touch wall pass may work as defender O_2 is behind the wall passer X_2. This leaves the passing lane open.

b. The wall pass can be delivered with the outside of the foot, curving the ball out of reach of a charging defender.

c. The wall pass can be chipped *over* the head of the interfering defender.

d. The dribbler can carry the ball beyond his defender and ignore his supporting teammate.

e. Other variations that involve the wall passer are:

1. In the first variation, the potential wall passer turns *blind side* to the defender O_2 and delivers a lead pass to X_1. (See Diagrams 9-17A, 9-17B, 9-17C, and 9-17D.)

Diagram 9-17A

Diagram 9-17B

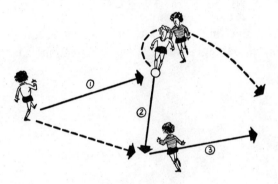

Diagram 9-17C

Diagram 9-17D

2. Now the wall passer X_2 one-touch back passes to X_1, who then delivers a through pass to X_2. X_2 turns *blind side* of the defender and races downfield.

3. This time the wall passer X_2 square passes the ball in front of X_1, who one-touch through passes the ball between the two defenders. Again, X_2 must turn blind side.

4. In final variation, X_2 draws his defender O_2 at the dribbler X_1. Suddenly, X_2 stops and turns so that he is running behind and away from the defender. Now X_1 has only to pass between his own marking defender O_1 and the ball-watching defender O_2.

As a final word, it should be obvious that the ratio of $2 : 1$ is a fragile relationship. Either defenders arrive to destroy it, or the participants tire in trying to hold it.

This first and final tactic advantage must be quickly seen by attacking players; taking advantage of this situation must be equally quick.

Chapter Ten

Three Attackers

Three Against One

WHILE THE TWO AGAINST ONE drills emphasized basic team combinations such as wall passing and takeovers, the three against one drills emphasize the basic concepts of support and use of space. At the same time the previous combinations are incorporated into the drills.

The Grid

In a marked area of 10 by 10 yards or 15 by 15 yards, three players are placed in corners of the grid or square. A defender is placed in the middle. Play begins (see Diagram 10-1) with X_1 in possession of the ball. Since he has a teammate to the left and right, he can pass in either direction. Thus, both players without the ball are in support positions. Initially, the defender exerts about a 50 percent effort.

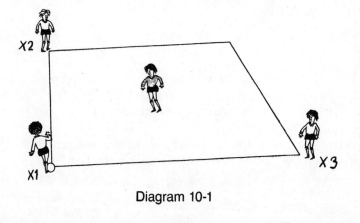

Diagram 10-1

The drill work begins with the ball being passed in a clockwise direction. Player X_1 passes to X_2. In Diagram 10-1, if X_2 has the ball, he can pass back only to X_1, as his teammate X_3 is directly behind the defender O_1. Player X_3 must move into the space of the empty corner to be able to support his teammate X_2. This move by X_3 shows that he understands the concept of *use of space*.

Now the ball should be passed to X_3 to continue the ball in a clockwise direction. X_1 must move into the vacant corner if the drill is to continue. The drill should continue until all the participants can demonstrate an understanding of the concepts of *support* and *space*. The defender should be replaced frequently.

Next, the ball should be passed in a counter-clockwise direction until the participants again demonstrate sufficient proficiency in the above concepts. Finally, the players can be instructed to pass in either direction each time they receive the ball.

Diagram 10-2

Open Space

The players are now ready to practice the same drill outside the grid.

1. In Diagram 10-3A, player X_2 has the ball and has support to his left or right. Assume that he passes to X_1. Then player X_3 must move to a position where he can support X_1 and allow him the option of passing to the left or right.

Diagram 10-3B shows X_3 and X_2 in support positions. Other support concepts can be developed from this position.

2. Assume that X_1 now passes to X_2. Player X_1 should move in the

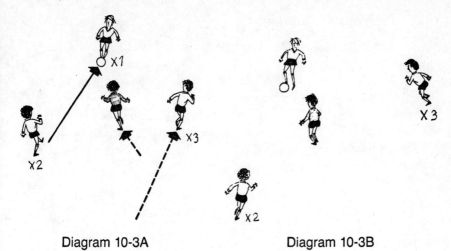

Diagram 10-3A   Diagram 10-3B

direction of his pass to give support to the pass receiver. If the defender O_1 does not move quickly to X_2, then X_1 can overlap X_2 to offer support on the far side of X_2.

This has the advantages of giving player X_2 quick support and also giving player X_3 a shorter run for support, since he can move to the position just held by X_1, rather than the longer run to the other side of X_2.

3. Diagram 10-3C shows X_1 on the overlap and X_3 replacing him. The players must practice this variation until they move quickly and smoothly to be in support positions for the player with the ball. Again, the defender must be replaced frequently.

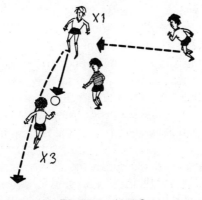

Diagram 10-3C

Functional by Position

The next step in the progression is to have the players drilled according to their actual positions on the right side of the field.

The fullback X_1 and forward X_2 are out by the touchline with the midfield player X_3 between them, but further in the field of play so that a triangle is formed. The defender O_1 is marking the forward (Figure 10-4), as he is the most advanced player. The drill begins by having the fullback pass the ball to the forward. (Why the fullback passes to the forward is explained under the section, "The Dutch System.")

Diagram 10-4

This pass must be delivered even though the forward is being marked. Both players practice playing under these conditions. In the beginning the defender is passive, so that the attacker learns to work with opposition.

The fullback moves forward following his pass (Diagram 10-5A). He moves in the direction of his pass for support, and he also begins an overlap of the forward. The forward passes the ball back to the midfielder and runs in the direction of his pass. This gives support to the midfield player and at the same time draws the defender away from the touchline creating space for the overlapping fullback.

The final step is to have the midfield player deliver a lead pass to the overlapping fullback X_1 (Diagram 10-5B). Now the midfield player runs to the near post to receive a cross from the fullback running into the corner with the ball. The wing runs to the far post and sets up on the 6-yard line.

(By now you should recognize the pass combination up-back-and-through, which was explained in Section II. More important, your *players* must recognize these pass combinations as they are developing. Then "running off the ball" is purposeful.)

Diagram 10-5A   Diagram 10-5B

The players should explore alternate variations of this play. They should find and practice the variations that work for them. The following are three that should be tried. They are suggested as a starting point for further variations.

1. In Diagram 10-6A the forward dribbles back toward X_3, the midfielder, while the fullback starts his overlap. The defender will have to follow to stay near the ball. Midfield player X_3 moves toward the dribbler and overtakes the ball. While the defender is briefly screened, the ball is passed to X_1, the fullback, who has been running the overlap. Now the fullback can dribble to the corner and cross to the forward, who turns and runs to the near post following the takeover by the midfield player. (See Diagram 10-6B.)

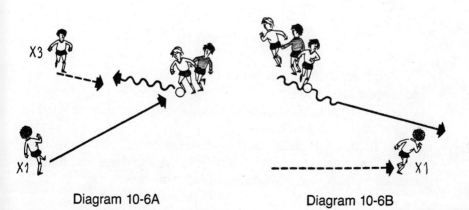

Diagram 10-6A   Diagram 10-6B

2. In the second option, the forward receives the ball from the fullback, passes back to midfield, and then the forward runs to the corner before the fullback can make the overlap (Diagram 10-7A). The midfield player now has three options:

   a. Pass to the forward if unmarked
   b. Pass to the fullback if unmarked
   c. Carry the ball himself to the goal

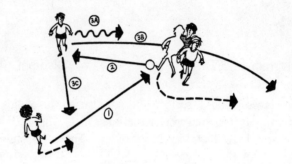

Diagram 10-7A

Diagram 10-7B

In all of these options, two attackers run to the goal—near post and far post. The drill is good for the physical conditioning of running to each post, plus the *mental* conditioning to see that the goal is attacked, near post and far post.

3. In the final option, the forward keeps the ball on the pass from fullback and begins to dribble away from the goal line. The fullback starts the overlap run, while the midfield starts the overlap run, while

the midfield player begins a run for the corner (Diagram 10-7B). Then the forward passes back to the fullback. The fullback lead passes to the midfield player, who is near the touchline running toward the corner. Variations are suggested according to the position of the defender. The attackers must learn to recognize each variation and react accordingly.

Practice Variations

Now that the players have executed the various combinations and understand the basic concepts, they are ready for the execution of these drills in a variety of groupings.

1. *Nine players.* Three groups of three players practice with one group attacking and another defending: one defender, one keeper with a small goal, and the final player resting. The third team rests and waits at the opposite end of the field.

The team of A, B, and C attacks defender X and keeper Y in Diagram 10-8. Teammate Z waits on the side. As soon as team X, Y, and Z gains the ball they will attack team K, L and M waiting at the opposite end. Meantime, team A, B, and C leaves the field and assumes the positions held by X, Y, and Z. This creates a perpetual three-against-one drill with one team attacking, one defending, and one resting. Furthermore, the attacking team can be instructed on *how* to attack; i.e., use a through pass, a wall pass, a dribble takeover, an overlap, etc. The players must learn to recognize the various combination situations, and also learn to *create* such situations.

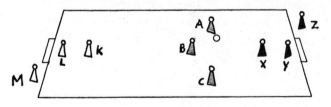

Diagram 10-8

2. *Six players and two goals.* This drill can be run for only three or four minutes, as it is very fatiguing. The team with the ball uses all three players. The defending team has one field defender, one goalkeeper and the remaining player is resting. The roles are reversed when the defenders win the ball. (See Diagram 10-9.)

3. *Six players—no goalkeepers.* The Dutch buildup concept can

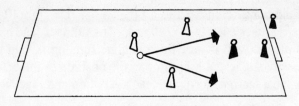

Diagram 10-9

be practiced by using six players. At one end of an enclosed area, perhaps 20 by 40 yards, is a team of three players against a single defender. At the opposite end an attacking teammate waits guarded by a single defender. When the long pass is delivered to the waiting teammate, two players rush to his support, creating a three-against-one situation, and attack the goal. (See Diagram 10-10.)

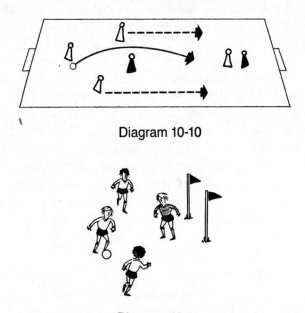

Diagram 10-10

Diagram 10-11

The ball is passed safely and under control in section A, while it is passed quickly and with risk in attacking section B. Then the direction is reversed with the buildup beginning in section B, and the rapid attack finished in section A. And so on.

4. *Four players—one goal.* Reduced to simple terms, this is three players attacking a single goal with one defender. The goal can be

attacked from either side. (Diagram 10-11). This kind of drill can be run only for a short duration, as it is most intense when executed correctly.

5. *With keeper.* Same as the above drill, except a goalkeeper is added. The attacking team still has the option of attacking from either side. This drill must be executed quickly, as time will help the defense to set up.

The Buildup from a Throw-in

As a variation, the players can be placed on the field to execute a buildup drill ending with a quick shot on goal.

Three players are placed on the defensive half of the field (Diagram 10-12.) One acts as a defender, while the other two prepare to go on the attack. A third teammate waits at the touchline with the ball. On signal, the third player throws the ball into play for safe buildup passes. These are followed by a deep pass to the forward at the other end of the field on the edge of the penalty area.

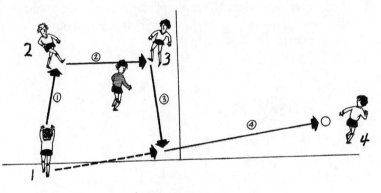

Diagram 10-12

Player #1 follows his pass downfield. The near attacker, #3, follows him. Player #4 has two options:

a. He can turn and shoot. Then the player running downfield takes his place and the drill is run again. The defender should be replaced after each execution.

b. Deep player #4 can hold and screen the ball for the player coming from behind (#1 in Diagram 10-12) and square pass it to him for a shot on goal.

After each of these variations has been run successfully, a

defender can be added to mark the deep man (#4 in Diagram 10-12). In both cases, the passer alone comes from behind to support the deep man receiving the ball. Then a second player moves forward from the defensive half of the field. This creates a drill of three-against-one in a buildup leading to a three-against-one in an attack on goal. The up-back-and-through is an obvious combination to be tried frrom this organization. A simple rotation will remove two attackers from in front of the goal, while two new players are added at the other end. A sweeper can be added to put more pressure on the attacking players.

The buildup. The man delivering the deep pass upfield *must* be facing the direction in which he is going to pass the ball. Avoid the situation where the passer must first control the ball, turn, and then survey the situation upfield before he can pass. The Dutch call the man facing upfield the "window" man. Consider the situation from the moment of the throw-in.

In Diagram 10-13, player #1 throws to #2 who passes to #3. The chances are that #3 is facing his teammate #2, and is not facing downfield as a window man. However, player #1 can start to run facing downfield and receive a square pass from #3 and then deliver the deadly deep pass to #4 downfield.

Diagram 10-13

Here, player #1 acts as a window man and passes downfield. This is also an example of a player moving from behind the defender to open space, as was illustrated in the three-against-one drill run in the grid and with the ball being passed in a clockwise direction. (This also shows that all parts *really do* fit together!) Diagram 10-14A shows another variation, the result of player #2 back passing to #1.

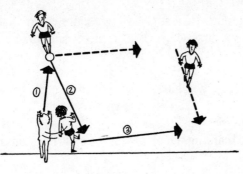

Diagram 10-14A

Player #1 passes to #3 who has run to the empty "corner" when he initially found himself behind the defender. Now player #3 can square pass to #2 running forward. Then #2, the window man, can pass downfield (Diagram 10-14B). Either a square pass or a back pass will give the ball to a window man. To review: The three-against-one drills teach:

1. Support for the passer and use of space to develop this support.
2. Practice of basic combinations such as wall passing, takeovers, etc.
3. Functional practice on the playing field.
4. Development of the Dutch buildup with the window man and deep player.

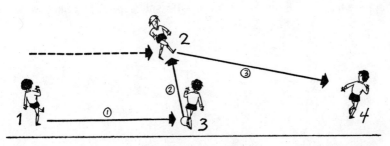

Diagram 10-14B

Three Against Two

In the ratio of three attackers against two defenders, the problem of maintaining numerical superiority is more complex now than in the three against one practice. It is also more game-like.

The Grid

Three players will have a difficult time keeping possession if they short pass the ball and run into the vacant corner. While players X_1, X_2, and X_3 are interpassing, the defenders O_1 and O_2 can take turns zone defending and marking the man with the ball (Diagram 10-15). Assume

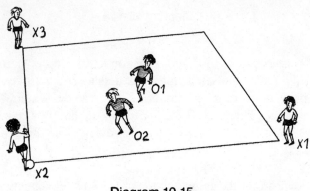

Diagram 10-15

that X_2 passes to X_3. The proper movement would be to run to the vacant corner where he can get from behind the defenders. But with two defenders in the middle, that pass may be impossible. Even a return pass to X_2 is threatened by the presence of defender O_1, who is supporting O_2 (Diagram 10-16A). The safest pass is one behind X_2.

Diagram 10-16A

This would have to be a soft pass that would not force X_2 to turn his back to his teammates. Eye contact must be maintained.

A second way to move the ball is by use of the takeover. Here X_2 carries the ball in a dribble in the direction of X_3, who moves to complete the takeover. This action will draw the attention of both defenders, with one going for the ball and the other supporting.

In Diagram 10-16B, X_3 has carried the ball back to where X_2 started and X_1 is open for the pass, as the defender has been pulled out of position by the action of the takeover. (See Diagram 10-16C.)

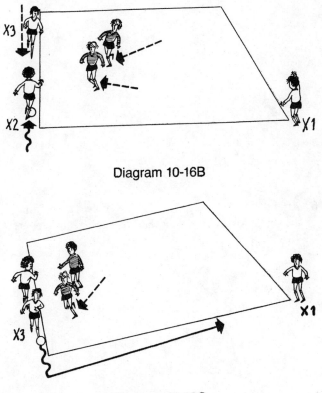

Diagram 10-16B

Diagram 10-16C

Player Movement Off the Ball

What about the movement of the attackers without the ball? There are two basic concepts that must be developed:

1. Move into free space away from the man with the ball.

2. Move toward the man with the ball to support him. The following sequence will demonstrate these concepts:

   a. This drill begins with X_1 passing to X_2. Since the two defenders are very near, X_2 passes behind X_1, which is the safest area for the pass. (See Diagram 10-17A.) Player X_3 stays away from the initial interpassing.

Diagram 10-17A

   b. After the return pass to X_1, player X_2 moves away from X_1. This is the signal for X_3 to move toward X_1 to give him support (Diagram 10-17B).

Diagram 10-17B

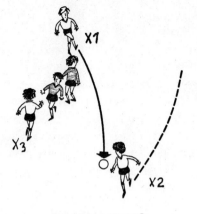

Diagram 10-17C

c. This short interpassing exchange plus the movement of the players without the ball forces the defenders to move so that the dangerous long pass can be delivered to X_2, who has moved to a deep position (Diagram 10-17C). It may be necessary to spend some time helping the players to recognize how these concepts are implemented.

There will be occasions when the two defenders try man-to-man marking instead of zone marking. This is particularly true when the attackers are working in a confined area, such as a corner of the field, by the goal line, or on the touchline.

If a defender tries to mark an attacker *without* the ball man-to-man, then such an attacker should try to isolate himself and the marking defender from the ball area. (Take him—the defender—away!) Now the true ratio is 2 : 1, and the two attackers should try to wall pass beyond the remaining defender. Thus, it can be said that one attacker "took away" his defender, and the two remaining attackers "walled out" the remaining defender.

Of course, if space allows, the attacker with the ball can exercise the option to go one-on-one with the remaining defender. This is an option that an attacker *must* be willing to take if he has the ball in the opponent's penalty area. In that area high risks must be taken.

After these concepts have been successfully demonstrated on an open field, the players can have additional pressure placed on them by practicing in a confined area. Begin in a space 40 by 40 yards, then reduce the area to 30 by 30 yards, and end an area of 20 by 20 yards.

Practice Oganizations

1. *Nine players and two small goals.* Three teams of three each are placed on a small field. One team of three attacks a goal defended by two field players and one player acting as a goalkeeper. At the opposite end, the third team waits to defend. When the active defenders win the ball, they immediately move to attack the opposite goal. The former attackers rest and prepare to defend. (See Diagram 10-18.) Instruct the players to deliver the long pass across the field as well as downfield. The same concepts are demonstrated in either direction.

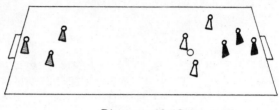

Diagram 10-18

2. *Eight players and two keepers.* This organization allows the players to practice the buildup at the defensive half, followed by rapid attack on goal. The attacker at the far end of the field is marked by a defender and a sweeper. His movement before he receives the ball is critical. He must move to the ball.

In Diagram 10-19, player X_1 moves to the touchline to receive the pass from X_2 after the buildup. He then dribbles to the endline. This initial move creates space for X_4 to come in from the other side. From the endline X_1 can long pass to X_4 or short pass to X_2 coming in from behind on the same side as X_1. As a variation, forward player X_1 can

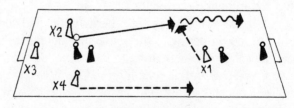

Diagram 10-19

run to the touchline, take the pass from X_2 and pass back to X_2. If X_2 gets inside one defender, the attack is reduced from three against two, to an attack of two against one. Dangerous odds in front of the goal! This drill with eight players is a favorite in Zeist, Holland.

Many basic concepts are demonstrated in this one drill:

   a. The buildup in the defensive half.

   b. The long penetration pass.

   c. The option of a long pass or a short pass from the endline.

   d. Switching. Continental play says that "you can't play without switching." Players X_1 and X_2 switch naturally in this drill.

   e. For defenders, it is imperative to defend on the side, not in the middle.

   f. One player stays away from the ball. Here it is X_4 coming from behind on the other side.

   g. One player stays nearby for support. Here X_1 and X_2 support each other.

No drill can be exercised without a clear purpose in mind. If one drill can demonstrate many basic concepts, its usefulness is greatly increased. (Don't jump from drill to drill if one drill will serve the same purpose.)

3. *Six players.* In a small area with two goals, three players attack two defenders. The third defender acts as a goalkeeper. When the ball is lost or a goal is scored, the attackers fall back to defend the other goal, with two players acting as field defenders and the third as a goalkeeper.

4. *Six players, one goal.* As a variation, the drill uses only one goal which can be attacked from either side (Diagram 10-20). Since one goal is used, the turnover of the ball does not give either team a chance to rest in the transition. The play tends to be more intense than in example 3.

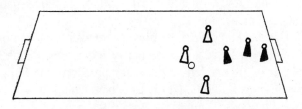

Diagram 10-20

5. *Five players.* In this variation, one player acts as the play maker for both teams (Diagram 10-21). He always works with the attacking team. Also, the ball must be touched by him when the ball changes to possession by the opposite team. This is excellent for midfielders, but it is also tiring for the middle player.

Diagram 10-21

6. *Five players in two grids.* In a grid of 20 by 20 yards, five players engage in a game of "keep-away" with three against two. While the three-player team has the ball, it is confined to this grid, which is surrounded by a 30-by-30-yard grid. When the two-man team wins the ball, the two players are free to play in larger 30-by-30-yard grid. If the three-player team wins back the ball, play is again restricted to the inner grid.

There are many variations that may be introduced into this game. The two grids can be increased or decreased in size according to the skill level of the participants. The three-man team can be restricted to one-touch passing, while the smaller team can be allowed free movement of the ball. Or, time each team to see how long each unit can control the ball. As with any other drill or practice game, make adjustments to be sure the drill works.

7. *Full team, half field.* The players are evenly placed on lines A, B, and C (Diagram 10-22). The keeper is in the goal. Play begins with the first player on line A delivering a long pass to midfield between the first player on lines B and C. (If the long pass cannot be delivered from the end line, the passer should dribble to the edge of the penalty area and deliver the pass from there.)

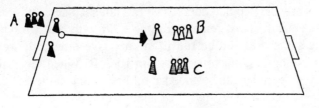

Diagram 10-22

Then player A becomes a defender while the first players from lines B and C collect the ball and move at the goal, play the ball by defender A and finish with a shot on goal.

The shooter goes to the end of line A, the defender and remaining player rotate to the ends of lines B and C. The players attacking the goal may need structure, such as being restricted to moving by the defender by a wall pass or takeover. Also, the defender may be told to give only 50 percent pressure until the drill is going well.

8. *Full team, full field.* A three against two drill can be run with the whole team on the length of the field. (See Diagram 10-23A.) Two

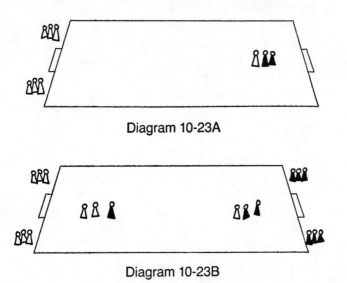

Diagram 10-23A

Diagram 10-23B

players enter the field from one side and interpass until they reach midfield. Then a long pass is made to a center forward who is marked by a marking fullback and a sweeper. The three players mount a swift attack against the two defenders. The two attackers then leave the field and the center forward remains on the field with the two defenders. Then the same drill can be run in the opposite direction, so that the completed diagram looks like Diagram 10-23B. When this drill is run smoothly, a defender can be added at midfield, so that the drill is one of two against one followed by three against two.

A final review of concepts to be developed in training three-man units:

1. All players must keep eye contact with the teammate in possession of the ball.
2. A hard pass can be played to the feet of an open teammate.
3. The ball can be played softly into space, so that eye contact can be maintained with the pass receiver. Normally, space is available *behind* a teammate, away from marking opponents.
4. The takeover should be tried by two players near each other. *Speed* must follow the takeover.
5. Attackers should try to play out one defender—isolate him—and then wall pass to him.
6. The ballcarrier should always consider the possibility of "going alone," i.e., taking on the defender 1 : 1.
7. Passes should be mixed long and short. There is a tendency to have three-player teams get "stuck" in a short passing game. The trainer must be alert to see that this does not happen. The long pass can be successfully played, but only with encouragement and concentration.

Finally, practice in 3 : 2 will produce many variations and player combinations. It should not be abandoned when it is achieving success. The trainer should encourage the players to become creative and imaginative in exploring the possibilities. It is not a simple drill; it is not easily mastered.

Chapter Eleven

Four Attackers

Four Against Two

FOUR ATTACKERS AGAINST two defenders is an excellent *training* ratio. Some coaches consider it to be artificial because the defenders have only half the number as the attackers. (An arithmetical progression would be ten against five—totally unrealistic!)

Many attack concepts and defense concepts can be taught from this formation. There is not enough defensive pressure to cause a breakdown of technique, so the tactical aspects of the game can be demonstrated clearly and efficiently.

Initially, this drill should be taught in a 15-by-15-yard grid. The four players with the ball are stationed in each corner, and two defenders are in the middle. Each group has two basic assignments:

On Attack	**On Defense**
1. Support the man with the ball by positioning a player to his left and right.	1. Mark the man with the ball. Cut down his passing angles. Restrict him to short, square passes. (See Diagram 11-1.)
2. Try to deliver the long through pass to the man diagonally opposite.	2. The second defender must support the marking teammate and must also prevent the dangerous through pass. (See Diagram 11-2).

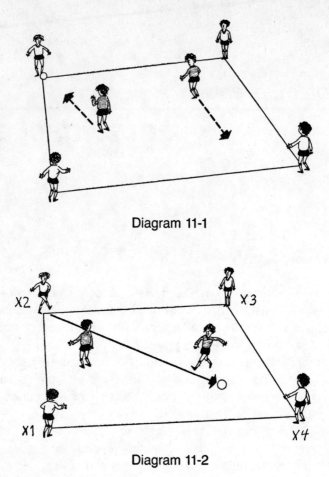

Diagram 11-1

Diagram 11-2

The Grid

The two support players should be encouraged to leave their corners and move closer to the player with the ball. If the four players remain in their corners, the drill tends to become too static. Also, since each side is 15 yards long, it may be necessary for the players to move closer together for good ball control. A few quick, short passes should split the defense so that the long pass can be made to X_4 in the opposite corner.

Open Space

Once these basic concepts are being demonstrated, the drill

should be moved to an open space. Here, the vital role of the deep man can be more clearly emphasized by having him run to a deeper position.

Once he has the ball, the two teammates X_1 and X_3 must rush to offer support to X_4 (Diagram 11-3A). It may be necessary for the three attackers in close position to interpass until the defensive unit is split. Once players O_1 and O_2 begin chasing the short passes, it becomes easier for X_2 to deliver the long pass between the two defenders. (This is another variation of "playing out" the defenders.)

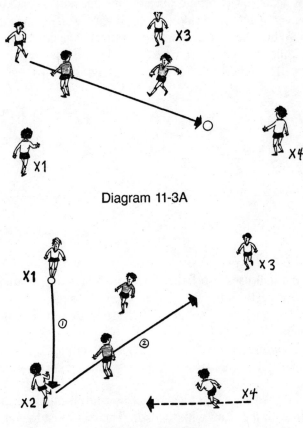

Diagram 11-3A

Diagram 11-3B

If player X_4 is unable to get free for the long pass, it is possible that either player X_1 or X_3 will move away from the group to assume the position of the deep man. In that situation, player X_4 must move in to assume a supporting role. This change still reflects a game-like situation (Diagram 11-3B), since often when the long pass cannot be delivered to a player positioned downfield, it is possible to make a long pass *across* the field to an unmarked fullback coming from behind on the opposite side.

Practice organization variations

1. *Twelve players*. Three teams of four each are organized on an area of about the width of a field. One team of four attacks another. The defending team has two field players plus one acting goalkeeper. The fourth player waits to the side. The third team waits at the other end of the field. When the ball is won, the defenders attack the far goal, four strong, while the former attackers replace the positions held by the defenders. The rotation continues. See Diagram 11-4.

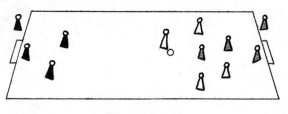

Diagram 11-4

2. *Eight players*. Two teams of four play each other. The team without the ball uses two field players and an acting goalkeeper. The fourth player rests on the side. When the ball changes sides, the former attackers fall back and defend the far goal with two field players and goalkeeper.

3. *Eight players and keepers*. Each defending team has two field players only. The other two rest, since regular goalkeepers have been added.

4. *Six players*. Two players act as neutral midfield players and play only with the team with the ball. The ball must be touched by at least one of the neutral players before a goal can be scored. Here team Y has the ball and attacks team O. The ball must go to X_1 or X_2 before a goal can be scored against team O. Following the goal, players X_1 and X_2 automatically become part of team O and attack team Y. The neutral players must be frequently replaced. (See Diagram 11-5.)

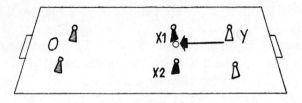

Diagram 11-5

Dutch Buildup Practice
(ten players plus goalkeepers)

At one end of the field four players begin the attack against two defenders. At the opposite end of the field two more attackers are being marked by two defenders. Assume that X_1 passes to X_2, who passes to X_4 (Diagram 11-6A). Player X_4 is facing downfield. He is the window man who delivers the long pass to teammate X_5 at the other end of the field. Players X_4 and X_2 rush forward to support X_5 and X_6 downfield. We now have a four-against-two situation at the defensive end of the field turning into a four-against-two situation in front of the goal. (See Diagram 11-6B.)

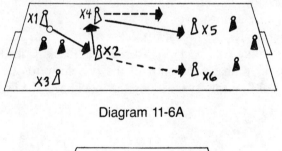

Diagram 11-6A

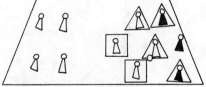

Diagram 11-6B

The four attackers must move quickly against the two defenders and score a goal. Assuming that the goal is scored, the buildup begins with two attackers who move upfield and become the two defenders. (This teaches attackers in the game, such as the forwards, to become defensive as soon as the ball is lost.) Now X_5, X_6, O_4 and O_3 are on the same team against X_2 and X_4. Any two of the attackers can join the group at the other end when the long pass is delivered. To help clarify the movement, attackers can be marked with triangles and defenders with squares (Diagram 11-6B).

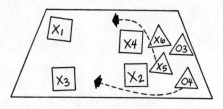

Diagram 11-6C

Now O_4 and X_6 join in the attack and help X_1 and X_3. Therefore, O_4 and X_6 become the defenders. The rotation continues in this fashion.

Functional Training

Arrange the players on the field by position and practice variations of four against two.

In Diagram 11-7A, fullback X_1 passes to forward X_3, who one-touch back passes to halfback X_2. Then the halfback X_2 lead passes to the overlapping fullback. Meantime, the two forwards have moved toward the goal to create space along the touchline. The drill finishes

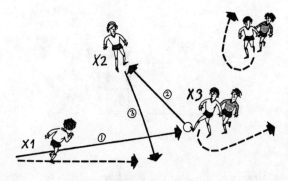

Diagram 11-7A

with the fullback crossing to the two forwards cutting to the goal (Diagram 11-7B).

Here the two forwards run a takeover ending with the lead pass to the overlapping fullback. The halfback cuts to goal.

To review: The two attackers who cross midfield become defenders when a goal is scored or the ball is lost. The remaining four players at that end of the field begin the buildup and finish with a long pass to the other end of the field. Two out of the four attackers who are nearest to midfield cross midfield to create a four-on-two situation in front of the goal.

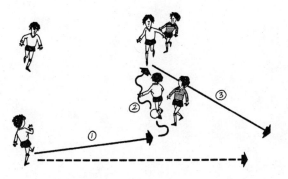

Diagram 11-7B

An easier way to run the drill is to keep the defenders as defenders, and the attackers as attackers. However, this defeats the purpose of the drill in two ways. To begin with, it forces an uneven distribution of work, since only four out of ten players are defenders. The pressure on them is continuous and fatiguing. Also, one purpose of the drill is to force attackers to switch to defense instantly when the ball is lost. This is accomplished only when the drill is run as designed.

Four Against Three

While numerical superiority is reduced in comparison to four against two, the basic concepts are the same. However, in many aspects this is an excellent grouping for training purposes. It involves one-third of all the participants in a regulation game. It also simulates the work of four fullbacks initiating the buildup against three opponents. While ball possession is demanded through a combination of short and long passes, and good running off the ball, the defensive unit can place game-like pressure on the attackers. As such, this drill may be considered to be the heart of the Dutch system.

In Diagram 11-8, players X_2 and X_3 maintain support positions to X_1, who must try to make the long pass to X_4. This long, through pass quickly places the ball in an advanced position and creates a dangerous threat to the opposition. This long pass is followed by a slowdown while X_4 waits for team support to arrive.

Diagram 11-8

Support players who are close to the player with the ball run in an *arc* to open space in order to be available for a pass. Normally, support players run in the direction of their pass.

Practice organization variations

1. In a grid without goals, play a game of keep-away four against three. The grid should be 40 by 40 yards and then reduced to 35 by 35 yards.

2. Run the same drill in an open area. *There must be a deep man at all times*.

3. *Twelve players*. Three teams of four play in a marked area. One team of four attacks a team of three defenders and a goalkeeper. The third team rests. Then the teams rotate positions. (This drill has been described in detail in previous sections.)

4. Goalkeepers can be added to the above variations.

5. Two teams of four play each other. The defending team uses three field players and one goalkeeper.

6. The above drill can be run with one goal. The goal may be attacked from either side.

7. *Seven players.* Two teams of three each play with one neutral midfield player. (The role of the neutral midfield player was detailed in a previous section.) The neutral player is the fourth man on either attacking team.

The buildup

The buildup can be practiced in a small field with two goalkeepers.

The buildup begins at one end with players X_1, X_2, X_3, and X_4 (See Diagram 11-9). At the other end of the field, players X_5 and X_6 are marked by two defenders and a sweeper. After the long pass to X_5 and X_6, two attackers move up to support the two forwards. The four attackers try to score against the three defenders. Following a turnover of the ball, the drill is run in the opposite direction.

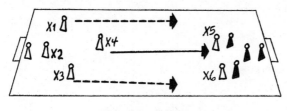

Diagram 11-9

Variations of four-against-three drills are very popular in Zeist, especially running the drills in an open area. When the players are comfortable with the drill, the attackers are limited to three-touch and then two-touch games. Finally, the four-man teams are asked to execute the various combinations learned in the two-against-one drills. These combinations include the wall pass, the takeover, and the through pass.

Many Dutch coaches consider this drill to be a prime vehicle for teaching tactics and technique. Drills with less than four on a side make the execution of the long pass difficult. For this reason, four-aside drills, such as four-against-three, are preferred to three-aside drills, such as three-against-two.

As a final note. ... We have had a Dutch National Youth Coach visit with our local youth team while they were being trained. The team was trained in the traditional drills of wall passing, etc., and they were run with the Dutch coach not showing any concern or particular interest. But when we started a 4 : 3 drill variation, his interest became obvious. He watched to see that there was a deep man available for the long pass. He watched for support left and right of the player with the ball. He drew an arc in the air to encourage curved runs off the ball. He called for the defenders to mark man-to-man *near* the ball, and to zone mark away from the ball.

He told us that he felt most at home with this drill. As a single drill, he felt that it made the greatest contribution to preparation for match play.

He felt that it was worthy of *many* hours of examination and practice.

We were not in a position to disagree.

Section IV

Tactics

THE FIRST THREE SECTIONS of this handbook placed heavy emphasis on various drills. These drills must serve a purpose, and at this point it might be best to *review* where we have been and why.

Let's begin with the game. There are normally three attacking parts to the game.

Buildup

When the defensive unit of a team gains possession of the ball, the buildup begins. The four defenders, in conjunction with the goalkeeper, begin to move the ball upfield through a series of short, safe passes. If the four defenders are marked by three attackers, a ratio of 4 : 3 is established. The presence of the keeper threatens to change this to 5 : 3. Section III covered training work to teach players how to deal with this situation. The buildup ends with the ball being carried or passed to the midfield area. At this point a "window man" looking downfield determines the next step in the attack.

(If all the fullbacks are tightly marked, then the keeper exercises the option of punting the ball downfield, where the odds must be reduced.)

In the buildup the goalkeeper can help advance the ball by forcing his teammates *out of the penalty area*. A turnover in the penalty area can be deadly.

Midfield

As the ball approaches midfield by way of the buildup, a "change" must occur. As players are marked in the buildup, space is created in midfield for this change. The Dutch use the word "wissel," or "change": change of pace, change of direction, change of design. The first obvious choice is to deliver long passes downfield or across field to bring about change—wissel. The 4 : 3 drill always threatens to end with the long pass.

Change is also created by combination play of the wall pass, takeover, give-and-go, or up-back-and-through. Such combination play carries the ball to the edge of the penalty area creating *danger!* All of the combinations were explained and practiced in Section II of this handbook. The long ball change—wissel must not be delivered *too soon*. The ball must be *received* in a dangerous place. We have seen teams deliver the long pass, as wissel, from the edge of their own penalty area. Such a pass is most often received at midfield—not a dangerous place. The ball must go quickly *through* or *over*, bridging midfield to bring a change of pace, distance, and purpose.

The final third

By the *change* the ball must arrive at the edge of the penalty area or *in* the penalty area. Such a ball is *dangerous* to the defenders just by its location. The attacker receiving the ball must be *willing* and *capable* of going 1 : 1 with the defenders. On occasion, the attacker must be willing to go 1 : 2 with the defenders. Section I covered the movement of the individual with the ball in preparation for going 1 : 1.

Thus, we have given practice for the major elements of the game. While the emphasis has been on the role of the attacker, the duties of the defender have also been covered, including personal marking and zone marking.

To summarize: The team that gains possession of the ball moves through three phases or steps:

1. The buildup in the defensive half with safe, sure passing, drawing in opponents to open up the other half of the field.

2. A quick change—by long balls played into a new area downfield or across the field, or a change of play by combination team work—the wall pass, give-and-go etc., to bridge the midfield area.

3. Players receiving the ball in the penalty area who are willing to go 1 : 1 to shoot and score goals.

So far these elements have been examined and practice work given, but there is still more to the game. Team formations and systems of play need further explanation. Tactics must be outlined. Set plays need to be given. Goalkeeper training must be considered as separate from training field players. The organization of a practice session must be detailed.

These areas and others will be covered in this final section of this manual. It will not be possible to pay attention to every detail, but we will try to cover the major areas that should be of concern or interest to the modern coach.

Chapter Twelve

Team Tactics

FOR THE DUTCH, tactics begin when a player is allowed a choice. This freedom of response should be allowed by the coach only when the player is *aware* of what choices are available, and when the player is *capable* of successfully executing any responses.

As an example, the tactical decision to wall pass can be made only by players who know how to wall pass. Once the technical ability to wall pass has been achieved, the coach must help the players to recognize *when* this skill should be executed. For this reason, controls are placed on small aside scrimmages that force this decision to wall pass. After wall passing becomes successful in a controlled scrimmage, the coach can have reasonable expectations of seeing the wall pass in a game.

There is no shortcut to success. The wall pass cannot be skipped in practice and then followed by its execution in a game; the wall pass cannot be called for in a scrimmage or game unless it has been successfully demonstrated in a drill situation. Choice follows control.

Having observed Dutch football on several occasions, our initial reaction was that American players did not know what tactical decisions to make during a game. We were convinced that the American players were possessed with 80 percent of the required techniques (or some other mythical percentage) and that the failure was tactical. This point of view was reinforced by the fact that our local club of 12-year-olds won constantly in Holland, our 14-year-olds won most of the time, our 16-year-olds won less often, and our 18-year-olds struggled to win. Thus, skills prevailed at the age of 12 and we won, while tactics prevailed at 18 and we lost.

Wrong!

The problem was then, and is now, that we developed a limited repertoire of techniques and skills at the age of 12 that allowed enough tactical variation to win. But this limited repertoire also limited tactics as the players grew, so that severe tactical limitations were being imposed by the limits of technique. Good conditioning and team spirit are not enough to win the modern game of soccer. *It cannot be stressed enough that technique limits tactics, or technique expands the tactical variations available to a team.*

For this reason, there are no secret tactics in soccer. The best tactics are available for the world to see and for any team to try. For the individual team and the individual player, the awareness of what tactical electives are available is limited only to the players' level of ability to execute the required technique and skills.

Thus, the Dutch speak of player position and systems of play as being part of an organic whole that stresses *movement* and *pace;* a gestalt if you like. Overlapping is part of this movement; switching from side to side is part of this movement; the buildup is part of the pace; the fast movement in front of the goal is part of the pace.

Obviously, the system fits the players!

The most popular system on the European continent is the 4-3-3. This means four defenders, three midfielders, and three attackers. The four fullbacks are subdivided into three marking backs and a last man or libero. The three midfielders typically form a triangle, with the center halfback behind the other two. He has duties that are 60 percent defensive. Should he move in front of the other two halfbacks, his duties become 60 percent attack The outside halfbacks should position themselves inside the wings. This allows direct passing from fullbacks to wings, and gives central support in front of the goalmouth.

Finally, the wings give width to the attack, and the center forward gives depth. Schematically, such a team may look like Diagram 12-1. With the flow of the game, this is seldom, if ever, seen on the field of play itself.

On occasions when the goal area becomes crowded, a forward is withdrawn and the system is changed to a 4-4-2.The two remaining forwards may be wings who continue to give width and create space in

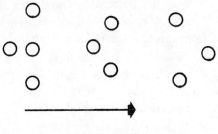

Diagram 12-1

the middle, or the two forwards may converge in the middle and act as twin strikers giving space on the flanks. When the 4-4-2 system uses twin strikers, the outside halfbacks can act as "false wings."

With the 4-4-2 there are different positions for the midfield players. The three most popular are shown in Diagram 12-2. The individual ability of the players and the strength of the other team will determine which system to use.

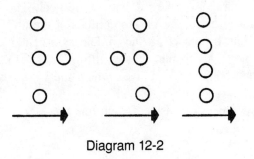

Diagram 12-2

Before specific tactics can be planned and developed, the team must be organized. Team organization should begin with the *defense*.

The four defenders *first task* is to stop the opponents from scoring goals. Defenders must be selected with close attention to their ability to mark players and stop an attack from either the flanks or the center. The strongest is placed in the middle—the stopper. The outside defenders, wing defenders, must have speed and the discipline to mark opponents and resist ball watching, or worse, ball chasing. The final defender is the last man or libero. He is free of specific marking duties, but must be prepared to go 1 : 1 with unmarked opponents advancing with the ball. The libero must organize the defense. He must work well with the keeper. If free, the libero must also be capable of taking the ball into the midfield when it is possessed in the defensive third of the field. Professional teams often convert midfield players into liberos. They must be smart players—capable with the ball.

The *second task* for defenders is to buildup when they possess the ball; their *third task* is to attack. Defenders should be selected in accordance to their ability to attend to these major tasks.

Select the midfield players according to specific team needs. The best midfielder must be able to make long runs, shoot well from inside the box and at the top (the 18-yard line) and also head well and take over a forward's position. As one Dutch coach said, "he must be a very good incoming player." The next best midfield player must be defensively-minded. He must be prepared to drop back and pick up unmarked players. He must be able to take over the duties of the libero when he moves into the midfield with the ball. The final midfielder must have ball control and be the play maker. He is the distributor.

The forwards must be skillful and fast. They must have mobility, creativity and courage to take the ball to the goal. The variations of forward formations are based on the abilities of the unit members. A skillful player can be placed in the middle as a center forward, and passes can be played to his feet. Less skillful, but faster players can be placed as wings; balls can be played where the wings can run on to them.

To review, the major tasks of each line are:

Last line:	defend	—	buildup	—	attack
Middle line:	defend	—	buildup	—	attack
Front line:	buildup	—	attack	—	defend

Once the team is organized and trained, it is possible to introduce team tactics. The best way to teach team tactics is to run a controlled scrimmage that involves the whole team with each player taking his field position. A six-against-four scrimmage on about two-thirds of a field will accomplish this purpose. Assuming that a 4-3-3 system is used, three forwards and three midfield players attack a goal defended by three marking fullbacks and a sweeper. A goalkeeper is added but does not count in the numbering (4-3-3) since he is not a field player.

For each scrimmage of this type, the defenders must be instructed to apply only about 50 percent pressure until the attacking unit exhibits a high degree of success. Then the pressure can be increased until the scrimmage is played under full pressure. At this point, the defenders should be allowed to counterattack to two small goals at about the two-thirds mark on the field. Each sequence should be started by a serve by the trainer or spare keeper.

Attacking Buildup Via the Center Forward

It must be assumed that any pass into the penalty area will have the pass receiver go one-on-one and try to score. However, passes received outside the penalty area should be treated as part of the buildup. In Diagram 12-3, the long pass is to the center forward. The

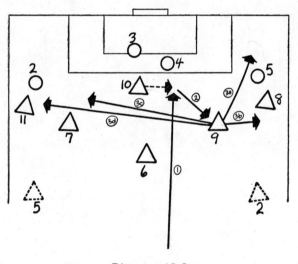

Diagram 12-3

"first look" by the window man should always be to the center forward as he is in the most advanced and dangerous position. In the sequence of the diagram, the center forward has moved to the right and passed back to the right midfield player, #9. The next pass depends on the kind of movement that takes place on the field. Player #9 can complete a give-and-go with player #10. A through pass can be made to #8 if he runs by defender #5. Or, #9 can wall pass with #8. On the other side a pass can be played to #11 or #7. Then, players #11 and #7 can run a crisscross and receive a pass with #7 running on the touchline and #11 cutting inside. The two outside fullbacks, #5 and #2, are included in the diagram, since it is implied that a fullback may be overlapping during any buildup situation.

The center midfielder must play most cautiously, fully prepared to be defensive in the event that the opponents counterattack.

Initially, the fullbacks should be instructed to mark the forwards at about 50 percent passive, while the attackers are learning to work together. Then the pressure is increased slowly.

A final word about the center forward. While Diagram 12-3 shows him moving to his right wing, his basic movement is up and down the field. First, he moves downfield against the opposing stopper and by his movements tries to push back on the stopper. This is called "checking in." (See Diagram 12-4.)

Diagram 12-4

In the process of "checking in" the attacking player creates space behind himself as he moves. When he "checks out," he stands facing the space that he just created. The ball can now be passed into this space. Obviously, the "check-out" movement must be sudden to catch the defender off guard. Thus the principles of pace and movement are being utilized to advantage.

Attacking Buildup Via the Wings

The second variation of the six-on-four scrimmage begins with a ball being served to the wing (Diagram 12-5). If the ball is played to the

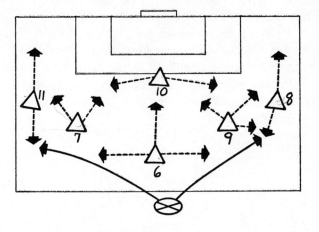

Diagram 12-5

right wing #8, who is supported by #6, #9, and #10, then any one of the combinations practiced in the two-against-one drills can be executed, including a wall pass, the takeover dribble, the give-and-go, and an overlap. Also, the wing can carry the ball to the endline and center the ball to a more central player for a shot on goal.

If the wing goes inside, then the opposite halfback must go outside to give the attack balance and prevent crowding in front of the goal. Thus, when #8 cuts inside, #7 must go to the far left touchline.

Again, #6 must assume a position that makes him the rear player so that he can become the prime defender in the event that the ball is lost.

The lines indicate the movement of the players in each position. The players must be given an opportunity to explore these lines of movement. The defenders again must be instructed to give 50 percent pressure, so that the attackers can learn to work together.

While movement of the wing players has been outlined, and the movement of the other players is keyed on the wing with the ball, the "first look" of the wing must be to the center forward. With the center forward in an advanced position a pass to him will quickly place the ball in a dangerous position.

On the other hand, if the center forward has withdrawn from an advanced position, such a move normally will create space that the wing can carry the ball into, or pass into for another player to shoot on goal.

Attacking Buildup Via the Halfback

In the final variation, the ball is served to an outside halfback who passes back to the center halfback, who has been coming up from behind. Fullbacks #5 and #2 are added (see the bottom of Diagram 12-6), as either of the fullbacks can be considered as a threat to attack by overlapping.

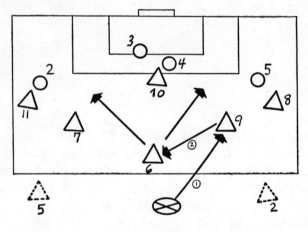

Diagram 12-6

Midfielders #7 and #9 must be prepared to change places, being sure that at least one of the two is always within reach of #6 with the ball.

The ball can be played forward as players change places. Also, combinations should be encouraged as outlined in the previous variations. The players must be prepared to move if they want to play. Again, the defenders begin with low pressure, and increase as the attackers learn to work together.

As the ball is played forward, the halfbacks must be prepared to assume defensive duties. They must position themselves to prevent a counterattack by the defenders. Defense is not an isolated position to be assumed by #6. However, the key to defense is found in how #6 positions himself. He must be in a position that is about 40 percent supportive of the attack and 60 percent prepared to be defensive. A similar defensive attitude must be assumed by the outside halfbacks when the ball is in the possession of the forwards.

Predictability

We have outlined several variations of the buildup from the long pass to:

1. Center forward
2. Left wing
3. Right wing
4. Left midfield
5. Right midfield

Each long pass was followed by sudden movement off the ball, passes to the switching players or combination play, and ended with a shot on goal or a defensive counterattack. The many possibilities must be explored by the coach and the players to allow for a maximum number of variations.

A team that does the same thing over and over again becomes predictable. The more predictable a team is, the easier the task of the defenders. That is why the deep pass must be delivered to five different players; that is why the combination play that follows must be varied. The wall pass must be changed for the give-and-go, etc.

For this same reason, the pace must be varied, with players making sudden unpredictable moves when they get close to opponents. Sudden movement, with and without the ball, will reduce predictability for the defenders.

Switching will prevent predictability. Wings that switch sides with each other cause defenders to have problems. The outside fullback will not like being forced to change sides. When the fullback solves that problem by switching assignments instead of sides, then the wing can withdraw and the outside midfield player can go forward to take his place, as *balance* must be maintained in the attack.

The point has been made, and it must be made again—players must be prepared to move, switch, change places, and overlap if they want to play the modern game of soccer.

Quadrant Drills

With all of the above drill variations, the underlying tactical principle is one of establishing numerical superiority near the ball. For some teams, this concept is difficult to demonstrate with ten or eleven players on half a field. The concept can become more realistic by playing on one-fourth of a field.

Have three attackers play against two defenders. A midfield player may join a wing and center forward in playing against two marking defenders. The task for each player is clearly defined and easily perceived. All the variations of attack can be introduced, including overlapping, wall passing, and back passing to center the ball. (See Diagram 12-7).

Diagram 12-7

The purpose of these drills, or any drills that are uneven in numbers, is to teach attackers to create numerical superiority and *use* it. The organization itself creates the numerical superiority; the drill allows players the opportunity to do something about it.

Tactics must be approached as a problem-solving process. The obvious problem is how to possess the ball and score a goal. The feeling among many coaches today is to allow the team to make a direct contribution in the problem-solving process.

Once the game begins, the coach is powerless to aid the team in making the necessary field adjustments to meet the unknown and survive. The more mature and independent team normally survives.

As stated earlier, *tactics* in the most basic definition is nothing more than the execution of one of a series of electives. The coach makes the team aware of what electives are available. A growing awareness of electives creates a tactically superior team.

Final Variations

A major problem in scoring is caused by having too many players in the box; each attacker attracts one or more defenders. Thus, four attackers commonly cause a total of ten players to be in the box; four attackers, four marking defenders, libero, and keeper.

Some coaches believe that a lack of scoring can be cured by increasing the number of attackers. *Exactly the opposite is true!* By withdrawing an attacker, more space is created in the penalty area, allowing better movement off the ball and greater opportunities for passing and/or shooting.

Withdrawing a forward may change the number of forwards, but the 6 : 4 remains the same with only a change in the placement of players. We have already examined the various formations of four midfield players. There remains only the position of the two forwards. To a large extent, the position of the forwards depends on the position of the defenders.

The two attackers can play wide as wings, while the midfielders exploit the center of the defensive unit. Or, the two attackers could pinch-in at the middle, leaving the flanks exposed to runs by the midfielders. Again, the attackers can play as one winger and one striker. Finally, they can play as twin strikers, in tandem, with the front player running to the corner, while the back striker runs to the near post.

Encourage your players to explore a variety of possibilities. Instruct the defenders on their roles. The attackers should try to penetrate the defensive formation. One or two accents can be placed on the drill-crossing, wall passing, playing out a defender in a 2 : 1 situation, etc.

Finally, when the 6 : 4 drill is running well, and the attackers are able to use their numerical superiority, add a fifth defender. The added pressure will make the practice more game-like, which is the essence of any practice.

Chapter Thirteen

Small Aside Games

GAMES PLAYED WITH a small number of players on each side simulate game-like conditions. They also have the advantage of giving the individual player many touches of the ball in a short amount of time. In fact, Eric Worthington, the English coach, has said that in seven or eight minutes of three aside, the individual player has as many touches of the ball as in a regulation game of ninety minutes duration. Also, players like to end practice session with a game-like situation.

During such scrimmages, ask your players to exercise certain skills such as wall passing. Also, place certain restrictions on the players, such as three-touch or two-touch passing. During the actual scrimmage your coaching instructions to the players should be minimal. Normally, there are short stoppages when instructions can be given. You would be better off to stop play to give instructions, rather than distract the players by yelling while they are trying to play the game.

Talk to your players, encouraging them and helping them. The best procedure is to concentrate on "coaching" ony one team in the scrimmage. Coaching should be done from the side of the playing field, not from the middle; you should be able to see all players at all times. The restrictions or controls should be minimal: one for low-level teams, and two or three for good groups.

Before organizing games or scrimmages, you should consider the following points:

1. *Organization*— What size? What shape? Square? Rectangle? How many goals? How many players on each side? Keepers?

2. *Rules*— All games must be played with a few simple, reasonable rules. How are goals scored; how are points awarded? Will the offside rule be followed? All participants must understand the rules of the game and how goals are scored.

3. *Purpose*—Any small aside game must have a purpose. There must be a purpose for the coach and the players. For the coach, careful observation is a primary purpose. This observation will allow the coach the opportunity to see if the team purpose is met. Equally important is the fact that observation will cause *change*—change in training, change in tactics, change in team system of play. Thus, a prime purpose is conducting a small aside scrimmage or game to allow the coach an opportunity just to watch the team perform.

4. *Player function*—Related to purpose is player function; that is, how the player is to behave on attack, on defense, with special emphasis on the transition between the two. You may want to watch how each team performs on the attack, or you may want to watch one team on both the attack and the defense.

5. *Opportunity for repetition*—If a combination (wall pass, etc.) is to be emphasized, provision must be made for repetition of the desired skill. If one purpose is to give the keeper practice in collecting air balls, then the attackers may be restricted to attacking the goal by headed balls only.

6. *Game-like conditions*—Any scrimmage must resemble a game. It must be a rehearsal for the "Queen of Soccer," the game. As part of the game-like condition, players must be *forced* to make choices: technical and tactical. In a real game, the coach will be powerless to influence these choices; in a scrimmage he must *observe* these choices. He must determine who is making good decisions under pressure. He must make note of those who succeed in the drill situation and fail under the pressure of the scrimmage. Only when game-like conditions are practiced can a coach determine what members of the team are ready to play.

Two Against Two

1. *Eight players*. Eight players can play in a grid as big as 25 by 25 yards, and if the players are skillful, as small as 15 by 15 yards.

Each corner is occupied by a stationary player who one-touch passes the ball to the field player who passed to him. Two players scrimmage against two within the grid. The corner stationary men are simply support players for whichever team has the ball (Diagram 13-1). After

Diagram 13-1

two minutes, the stationary corner men switch with the field players. This organization allows for many variations. As an example, the corner man can be instructed to wall pass only. Points can be awarded, such as one point for a wall pass with the corner and two points for *on the field* wall passes. Played properly, this is an intense and fatiguing organization, so that the field players must be replaced frequently. The larger the grid is, the more the players are conditioned. A smaller grid places more demands on technique. Some variations or rules of play are:

a. One-touch passing by field players to neutral corner men.

b. One-touch passing from the neutral corner men.

c. Wall passing—in field or with corner players.

d. 1-3 combination pass (pass from one field player to corner player, one-touched to the second field player).

e. Air passing.

f. Points assigned for any of the above.

   2. *Six players*. In an area 40 yards long two players play against two. Post a stationary player at each end of the area. The team with the ball may pass to the stationary player for points. The stationary player

must one-touch pass back to the same team, which now reverses direction and attacks the opposite end. (See Diagram 13-2.) As the

Diagram 13-2

players get better at this and the passing improves, the distance from end to end should be reduced until the playing distance is only 25 yards long. The intensity increases as the distance is reduced.

3. *Six players.* Another variation with six players can produce a game to two against two that is converted to four against two.

In a small marked-off area, two players play against two opponents (Diagram 13-3). Small goals are at each end of the field. Running along each touchline is an "extra" player. He never enters the field itself, but remains on the touchline. He is instructed to one-touch pass to the same team that passes to him. Furthermore, when a team gains possession of the ball, it must pass to the neutral extra man before scoring a goal. Thus, the organization forces an attacking team to use its wings and the width of the field. As the players become skillful, the neutral wings can be given special instructions, such as passing 1-2. That is, the pass received by player #1 is one-touch passed to teammate #2. Or, the wing man can be told to pass to the other touchline, etc. The use of a neutral player on the touchline is very popular in Holland. The team gaining possession of the ball is given immediate numerical superiority while at the same time forcing width to be used in the attack. With the extra players available for support, the field players should be encouraged to wall pass. While other combinations are possible, the wall pass should be the most practiced combination.

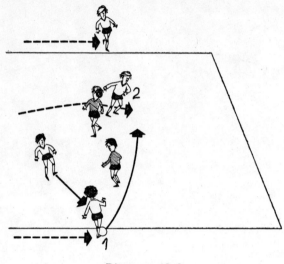

Diagram 13-3

Three Against Three

1. *Small area, no goals.* In a grid 25 by 25 yards or 20 by 20 yards, two teams of three each play a game of "keep away." The object of the game is to keep possession of the ball. At first, the ball will be turned over to the other team often in a short amount of time. As the players become more accustomed to the game, possession time will increase. Then points can be gained by making combinations, such as wall passing, takeovers, overlaps, etc.

2. *With goals.* Two small goals, without keepers, can be added to the same space as used in #1 above. The objective switches from possession to scoring. If two points are given for a goal, then one point can be given for field combinations such as wall passing. The goal area should be a yard or a yard and a half wide. If the players tend to cluster directly in front of the goal, width can be encouraged by making the goals triangular. This will force more shots to be taken from the side. (See Diagram 13-4.)

Diagram 13-4

3. *Wings added*. By lengthening the field to 40 yards, a neutral wing can be added to each touchline. The same rules apply as above: the neutral player cannot enter the field itself, and must one-touch back, etc. This creates a good five-against-three situation. The game can be made more interesting by allowing a second goal to be scored from the opposite or backside of the goal. Also, adding a *second* goal to each end will cause more long ball passing. Controls can be added, such as scoring by heading (most difficult), instep shooting, etc.

Four Against Four

1. Again, a game of keep away can be played in a grid that is 40

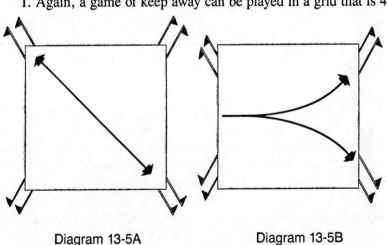

Diagram 13-5A   Diagram 13-5B

by 40 yards, or 30 by 30 yards; all of the above rules and variations apply.

   2. Two small goals can be added, or four goals can be used. If four goals are used, three designs can be considered.

   In Diagram 13-5A either the two adjacent goals can be attacked, or the two opposite goals can be attacked. The purpose will determine which is to be used. Diagram 13-5B is popular for creating width. Any two-goal design will cause the ball to be changed often ... wissel.

   3. Two neutral wings can be added to the touchline (Diagram 13-6). The neutral wing is always part of the attacking team. He can

Diagram 13-6

never be offside, but should try to stay even with the ball, when it is on his side. The neutral wing must work to become part of the attacking team. He must anticipate where a good pass must be made. He must anticipate what place on the touchline is most supportive. He must *prowl* in anticipation, rather than stand and wait.

Five Against Five

   The emphasis must now shift. A libero should be used by each team. The remaining four players on each team mark their opponents. Now the role of the libero must come into clear focus. Therefore, the libero must be rewarded for going forward. The midfield should be marked across the field of play. Then a point system can be established involving the libero. It can be a simple system or a more complex one. Some examples will demonstrate the kind of rules that can be made.

Diagram 13-7

1. If the four marking players are beyond midfield, but the libero is not, then a goal scored does not count.
2. If all five players are beyond midfield, the goal is worth a single point. If the libero scores, that is worth two points.
3. If the opponents score before all five players have returned to the defensive half of the field, the goal is worth two points. If the libero is not back on defense, the goal is worth three points.

This variation may not last more than three minutes, if well played. The ideal time is not more than five minutes.

Six or Eight Aside

For six aside, use about two-thirds of the field. Use the regular goal area at one end (with the keeper) and two small goals at the other end, perhaps 2 or 3 yards wide. A full field can be used for eight aside. By playing eight aside instead of eleven, the players must do more work. The work-rate demand is much higher. Poor technique is much more observable, as are good tactics. Movement off the ball is much more observable and critical to the game's outcome.

A short scrimmage of eight aside should quickly tell you about your team's strengths and weaknesses. Encourage players to play with intensity of movement, changing places, using combinations, changing the pace, and remaining unpredictable. When play becomes a predictable routine, action must be stopped ... at once.

A Final Word

With any of the above scrimmages, always begin with low pressure. As the game gets better through skill and understanding, pressure can be added. Give options to the players to help them make tactical decisions about running, passing, using space, and building up pressure. You must *control* the scrimmage and the tactics used in the scrimmage. Don't throw out the ball and become a spectator. You can control the scrimmage in many ways:

1. The buildup in the defensive half—safe passing—use of the goal-keeper. Try using ony 50 percent pressure by defenders in that area of play.
2. Combinations—No goals allowed before a wall pass, a takeover, or other combination.
3. Overlapping by a defender on the side opposite the ball. This is a good way of getting on the blind side of a defender.
4. Carrying the ball to the endline and passing back on an angle. This will stop bad angle shooting.

Players will respond to a coach's demands.

A scrimmage may be a type of reward for the players; it is a form of homework for you, the coach. You must study carefully to find out what future work needs to be done. You must list the needs in order of priority—what needs the most work down to the least. The list must be revised frequently.

Finally, a soccer season is a long time. Problems will not be solved overnight, or in a week. Some problems will not be solved in a season. They must all be approached one at a time. Therefore, the controls in a scrimmage should be limited; don't put half a dozen restrictions on play at one time. Decide what needs to be stressed and stress only it ... passing, shooting, ball control, etc. Do not stress passing *and* shooting *and* ball control. The players will not respond!

Chapter Fourteen

Circuit Training

CIRCUIT TRAINING is a weekly pre-season training activity in Europe, which can last from six to eight weeks. Circuit training is done with the ball, through easy exercises, to develop techniques of passing, trapping, dribbling, etc. Without the ball, the training emphasizes conditioning, such as speed, power, strength, jumping coordination, etc.

The circuit is usually a series of stations placed on a field. Each station calls for one specific task by a player, passing, heading, shooting, etc. The player moves from station to station performing the different tasks at each stop. Normally, the stations are arranged in a rough circle, which gives the sequence its name—circuit training.

To make each task more meaningful to the participants, the technique of *interval training* is used. This technique creates an intensive loading of certain muscles for a specific amount of time followed by a period of rest or relative rest. Repeated exercises of intense work followed by a short rest period will help a soccer player to increase his endurance, speed, and the specific skills being practiced.

Each station can be designed to accommodate one or two players at a time. The most popular way is to have each station occupied by two players. One does the exercise while the other rests and records the results of the performer. Then the positions are reversed.

This means that the work interval and the rest interval are the same. Also, the sequence of stations can be organized so that one task is difficult to perform and the next is relatively easy. If each exercise lasts for one minute, followed by a minute of rest, the entire circuit will be easy to organize and run. Two-man teams of players would spend two minutes at each station.

If a team has sixteen players, a circuit of eight stations will keep the whole team occupied.

Certain rules should be followed in creating a circuit:

1. Each station should serve a purpose.
2. Try to combine strength and coordination.
3. Separate stations that exercise the same muscle group a second time.
4. There can be more stations than participants; all stations do not have to be used at once.
5. Work *can* be done with two, three, or four players at each station.
6. Use at least six stations.
7. Play soccer after one round.
8. If maximum response is called for, ask for only two or four repetitions per station.
9. If minimum response is needed, ask for eight to ten responses per station.
10. Check the heartbeat. There is no positive training influence in a high pulse situation.

The following example has eight stations, which allow sixteen players to train at once.

1. Set up two walls, perhaps two tables or two benches. The two players start at opposite ends and run and wall pass to their left, collect the ball, turn, and repeat the pass as many times as possible in one minute. They then move to station #2. One point per pass. (See Diagram 14-1.)

Diagram 14-1

2. Two players duel in a game of one-on-one with one goal about a yard wide. The goal can be attacked from either side. (A second goal can be added 20 yards away.) (See Diagram 14-2.) After one minute, move to station #3. One point per goal.

Diagram 14-2

3. Two players set up a give-and-go combination ending with a through pass. Then they reverse direction and repeat for one minute as often as possible. Each player gets one point per through pass. Then move to station #4. (See Diagram 14-3.)

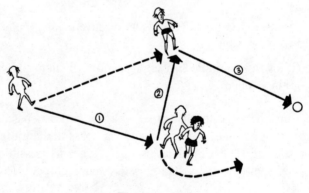

Diagram 14-3

4. Two players start with a ball at a "gate" 20 yards apart. (A gate is a metal mini-goal, 30 inches long and 15 inches high.) On signal, they pass through the gate, dribble to and *around* the next gate, pass through and repeat in the opposite direction. When the player passes through a gate, he must jump over it. Each pass through a gate is one point. After one minute, they move to #5. (See Diagram 14-4.)

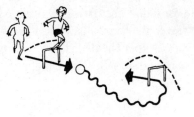

Diagram 14-4

5. Stand in front of the goal on a designated spot (close in for young players; further out for older ones). On signal throw the ball in the air and head into the goal. Retrieve the ball and repeat for one minute. One point per goal. Then move to station #6. (See Diagram 14-5.)

Diagram 14-5

6. Two small walls are set up 30 yards apart, facing each other. The player dribbles and passes to the wall, collects the rebound, turns and does the same to the opposite wall. One point per rebound. The wall can be a turned-over table, the size of a bridge table. Then move to station #7. (See Diagram 14-6.)

Diagram 14-6

7. From the 18-yard line, the player shoots two balls into the goal-mouth. He then retrieves the two balls, returns to the 18-yard line and continues until his time is up. (The distance can be reduced for younger players.) Then move to station #8. (See Diagrams 14-7A and 14-7B.)

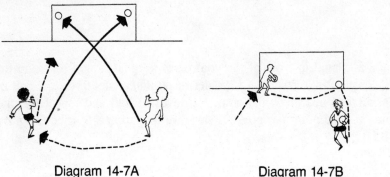

Diagram 14-7A   Diagram 14-7B

8. From a designated spot the player throws balls to a target, such as two corner flags, 1 yard apart. This throw-in activity stresses accuracy and distance. The thrown balls are retrieved, and the activity is continued until time is called. Then move to station #1, as in Diagram 14-8.

Diagram 14-8

Once the circuit is completed, allow a general rest period; then the circuit can be run a second time. Compare scores for each round.

This is but one example of circuit training. The advantage for a coach is that is supplies him with a good organization to give practice to those skills that appear to be weakly executed by the team. As the specific skill areas are strengthened, the players' endurance and speed also should improve.

There are endless variations. As an example at station #6, we said, "The player dribbles and passes to the wall, *collects the rebound, turns,* and does the same to the opposite wall." How can a player collect the rebound?

1. He can trap it with the inside of his foot and turn.

2. He can use the outside of his foot and turn.

3. He can drag it with a wedge trap, using the inside of his foot, and make a ¾ turn.

4. He can let the ball roll between his feet, turn and run onto the ball.

Thus, the coach can control the technique being practiced at each station. The entire circuit can be repeated several times at each session. Six repetitions is considered maximum. Consider this time factor:

Six stations—Allow 1 minute at the station and 30 seconds moving between stations; then you have one round of stations in 9 minutes. For the next 9 minutes the participants play soccer, such as 3 : 3. Consider this one circuit repetition. Do this six times and the activity has used up 108 minutes; it is one full training session. And what a session! How did the participants do the sixth time in the circuit of stations as compared to the first? Better? Worse? Was one station very strong from first to sixth repetition? One weaker? What does that tell you? Use circuit training with *purpose.*

A Word About Conditioning

The national staff of the United States Soccer Federation strongly recommends the "all ball" approach to soccer training. This is sound advice for several reasons.

With the shortness of the average season, it is imperative to use the ball in training as much as possible. This gives the advantage of developing technique at the same time that conditioning work is being done.

Also, work is more attractive when it is done with the ball Players do not find the drill work to be a chore if the ball is used. It is associated more with "fun"; the task is easier to perform.

The Dutch have much the same kind of attitude. The very first drills, dribbling and turning, demonstrated how conditioning was introduced by making the circle of players larger and larger. In movement education, it was seen that small space placed demands on technique, while increased space placed demands on conditioning.

However, during the total training program, there are some jumping drills that are unique and seem to help in the development of strength, skill (to jump) and endurance.

As such, the following drills may be of value as a pre-season exercise.

Organization: Place the players on one side of a grid. This grid can be 20 by 20 yards, or 30 by 15 yards and even 20 by 10 yards, depending on the number of players and the drill.

The duration of each drill will depend on the ability and conditioning of the team.

1. Hop in place. A short relaxed hop is followed by a high jump. Hop with both feet together, and then one foot at a time.

2. With both feet together, hop forward from one side of the grid to the other. Count the number of hops made by each player. The winner is the one who made the least number of hops.

3. Hop in place, first one foot, and then the other.

4. Hop from one side of the grid to the other advancing from one foot to the other. To prevent this from becoming a run, we tell the players that they are to imagine that they are crossing a steam, jumping from stone to stone.

5. Take running jumps across the grid.

6. Around the grid, run the leg of one side, and take running jumps along the next leg. Repeat the pattern several times.

7. Place seven rows of balls across the grid. Have the players hop across one foot at a time, landing next to each ball as they move. Then increase the distance between the balls, forcing the jumps to be longer. See Diagram 14-9.

Diagram 14-9

8. Divide the team into two groups—Team A and Team B. In the middle of the grid place two players who each hold a stick or pointer parallel to the ground. The stick should be held at about the mid-point of the thigh. Then run a relay race. In turn, each player runs from one side of the grid to the other, jumping over the stick as he runs in each direction. Then he turns, runs back, again jumping over the stick, and when he returns to the starting point, a new player begins the next leg of the race.

Several years ago we asked a Dutch junior player from North Holland how his team prepared for the season. He said that they jumped over hedges. We thought he was kidding.

How to Adjust Drills to Make Them Work

In circuit training drill work, or drill work in general, the youth coach is often faced with the problem of drills that don't work. How can they be changed to make them work? A related problem is the drill that works too well. The participants don't seem to be getting any training benefit from the work. How can it be made harder to perform?

There is an approach to physical education that is used in America and Europe that helps to answer these questions. This approach is called *movement education*. A review of the basic elements of movement education will reveal how soccer training is aided. These elements are:

1. *Time*. There are many factors related to time. Duration of time is one factor. How long can one team possess/pass the ball without interception? Repetition in a given time is a second factor. How many times can an exercise be performed in a minute? Thirty seconds?

Also related to time is pace—sustained, fast, slow, sudden change.

2. *Space*. There are many factors to consider with space. The larger the space the more the emphasis is placed on conditioning; the smaller the space the more the emphasis is placed on technique. Young and inexperienced players need more space to have time to run to a ball passed at a bad angle. Players with good technical skills can be placed in a very small space, forcing a fast reaction to every situation to develop *quickness*. Also related to space, not for the player but for the ball, is the emphasis placed on range—how far to pass the ball; direction—where to pass the ball; and level—at what height the ball should be passed.

3. *Force*. This relates to how the ball should be struck: minimum force, light, hard. It deals with passed balls and headed balls.

4. *Flow*. A drill should be practiced until the participants develop a good rhythm or flow. As an example, three attackers who are experienced should be able to pass the ball around one defender. They should be able to do this is an open area—free flow or within a grid-bound flow.

Once this easy flow is achieved, the drill should be made more diffcult so that the participants work harder to achieve a flow. This can be done by changing one of the other elements. The *time* that a player has with the ball can be reduced by playing two-touch or one-touch soccer. The *space* can be reduced by demanding a higher technical skill. The *force* of opposition can be increased by introducing an additional defender.

There are other elements to movement education. All of them cannot be reviewed here, as this is a very large subject worthy of a separate bibliography by itself. We will end with a simple flow chart (See Diagram 14-10 on the next page) that will show most of the basic elements of movement education. A good teacher must make himself aware of these elements in detail.

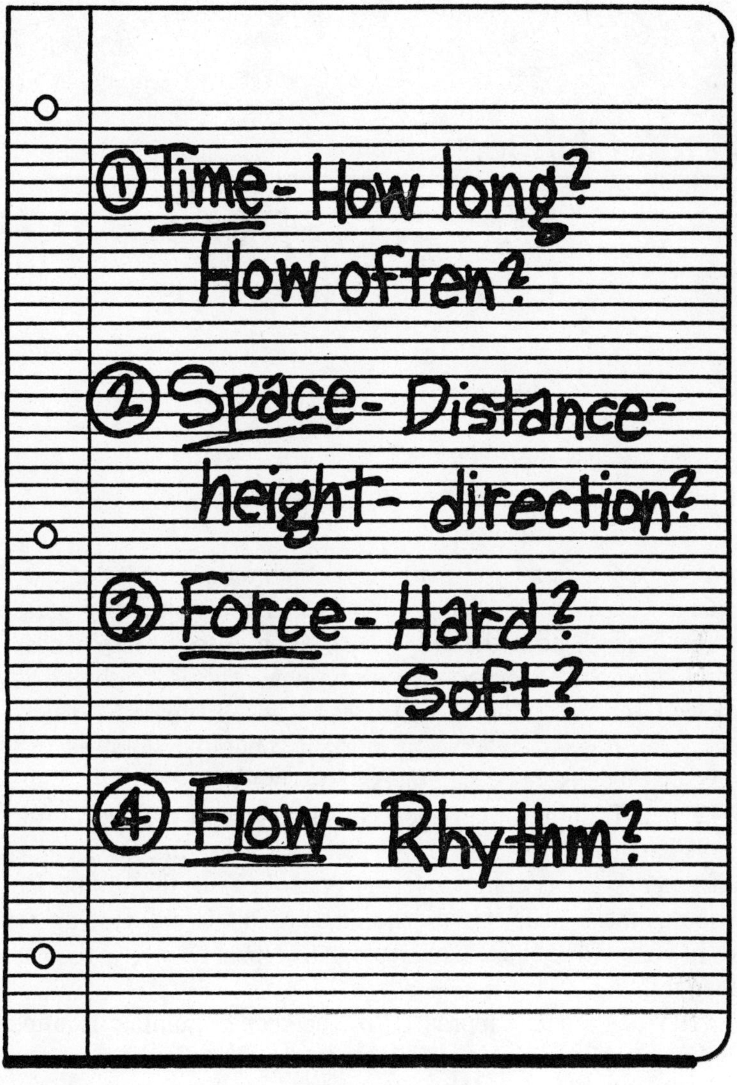

① Time - How long?
     How often?

② Space - Distance -
     height - direction?

③ Force - Hard?
            Soft?

④ Flow - Rhythm?

Diagram 14-10

Chapter Fifteen

Goalkeeper Training

THE POSITION OF THE GOALKEEPER is both unique and singular; it is unique because he can use his hands in his own penalty area, and singular because he is the only player allowed to use his hands. The training of a goalkeeper should be functional. That is, he should always work with the ball in an area that serves as a goalmouth. If need be, two corner flags can serve as uprights, but the point is that the goalkeeper needs his "landmarks" to practice and function as a goalkeeper. Training on an open, soft grassy area will not do this.

It has been said that for 80 percent of the time in a game, the goalkeeper simply collects loose balls behind the fullbacks and distributes these balls to start the attack. This is an amazing fact, if true, in view of the abuse that many goalkeepers receive in the name of proper training.

The continental approach to goalkeeper training is aimed at technique, not conditioning. The thrust of practice is not to wear down or wear out the keeper. Nor is the purpose to frustrate the keeper by serving him balls that he cannot stop or hold. The Dutch say that in goalkeeper training it is easy to score. But the purpose of goalkeeper training is not to make the keeper look bad and the trainer look good. (While in Holland we saw one experienced trainer "burn" the keeper by putting hard, sudden, wide shots into the goalmouth. While the keeper flopped on the ground, other coaches clucked, saying that the offending trainer was showing poor form.)

The proper training of a goalkeeper is a subject worthy of an entire book. It is not our intention to even pretend that all aspects of keeper training will be covered here. Rather, we would like to make some comments about technique so that the proper purpose is defined and understood.

Diagram 15-1A

Diagram 15-1B

Begin by placing the keeper in the goal. Actually, he should cover the goalmouth by running on an arc in front of the goal. Tall players can run in a larger arc than short ones. They must stand close enough to stop high balls that might slip in just under the cross bar. But also, they must stand in front of the goal line, ready to run to a loose ball, and block an attacker's view of the open goalmouth. The size of the arc is dictated by practice and experience. See Diagrams 15-1A and 15-1B.

The keeper must consider three elements:

    a. The angle of the ball

    b. The speed of the ball

    c. The distance from the goal

Ground balls

The training begins with ground balls served by the coach. The player must move to the ball, reaching out with his hands to pick up the ball. This is a key point. If the hands are held against the shinbones, there is a chance of a slap rebound of the ball. Then control is lost. Instead the hands must be held *away* from the body. Then the space between the hands and legs acts as a cushion and reduces slap rebounds of the ball. When the ball is caught it is held next to the body. See Diagram 15-2.

Diagram 15-2

The ground balls can be served directly at the feet. Then the speed can be increased and the distance changed. When the keeper is comfortable with these ground balls, the trainer can change his position so that the ball is approaching at different angles. Finally, the ball can be served softly to the left and right of the keeper. These balls must be played softly so that the goalie has a chance to place his body behind the ball. Again, he must have an opportunity to get *every* ball.

Balls may be served that force the keeper to kneel when reaching for the ball. However, when the knee goes down (the outside knee, always) it must not touch the ground. The player's balance must be maintained from a crouched position. No balls should be served that force diving at this time.

Air balls

The players should now be served balls that are placed higher and higher on the body—knees, stomach, head high. Again, there can be variation in speed, angle, and distance. The player must have practice in reaching for the ball and pulling it to his body. The serves continue with balls that the player must reach for, but do not require jumping.

At this point, the serves can be made to the left or right of the keeper, always testing his reach short of jumping or diving. Encourage the keeper to try harder for each save. He must learn the limits of his reach. He must learn to judge how to go forward and take his hands to the ball. Balance must be maintained.

Balls can now be served over the head that force jumping. Each catch must end with the ball held on the chest and the player on his feet. With the ball served from different angles, the keeper quickly finds the path of his arc in front of the goal as he tries to keep a maximum path and still protect the goal from high balls.

Diving

A goalkeeper will dive successfully if he is coached to the final step-diving and maintains proper confidence through the progressive steps.

1. *Kneeling*. The goalkeeper starts in a kneeling position and falls, arm extended, no ball, left and right. This should be a simple fall. The player should not try to *throw* himself to the ground. After the move is made with confidence, the actual ball can be used. The player should try to pull the ball to the chest while still in the air. Only repeated practice will enable the player to learn how to hold on to the ball and cushion his fall. Again, the trainer should vary the angle, distance and speed of the ball.

2. *Squat*. Next the player begins from a squat position. The trainer must test the player for the limit of his jump. Again, the ball should be pulled in while in the air. Players may reveal a weak side in jumping. By going one step at a time, failures or weaknesses can be isolated, analyzed, and corrected.

3. *Crouch*. The next step in diving is to have the player crouch, with a balanced stance, and dive to the left or right. From here it is a simple step to standing and diving. If at any point the player loses his concentration or confidence, just move back a step until execution is achieved.

In diving, when the goalie moves *with* the ball, instruct him to move *against* the ball.

Punching

The player must learn to punch first with two fists held together. The thumbs must be held outside the fist. It is common to break a thumb if it is held in the fist. The body should be arched like a wound coil to give body thrust to the punch, as shown in Diagram 15-3.

Diagram 15-3

Initially, the ball should be punched back in the same direction from which it came. The ball should be served in variations of angle, speed, and distance but within an area where it can be punched with two hands (fists).

The final objective of the keeper should be to punch the ball out on an angle. If the ball comes in from the right, it should be punched out on the left, and vice versa. At first it may not be clear to the keeper why the ball should be punched out on an angle. A passive attacker should be stationed in front of the keeper. His presence alone will cause the keeper to understand why balls must be punched at an angle.

The last step in punching is the use of one fist. High balls from the side should be punched on to the other side with one fist. Balls that are played to the extreme of a keeper's range can be punched or deflected with one hand.

One-on-One

Sooner or later every goalkeeper comes face to face with an opponent who is dribbling in for the unguarded shot on goal. The keeper must run rapidly to face the dribbler. As he approaches the dribbler he must keep his arms wide to reduce vision. He may even back up after running out. As he nears the ball to block the shot, he assumes the posture of someone trying to catch a chicken. Seriously! (See Diagram 15-4.)

Diagram 15-4

After the goalkeeper begins technique practice, various tactical aspects can be discussed and implemented. It won't hurt to have the keeper stretch out on the ground to find the spot that allows the near post to be covered from a maximum range. The keeper will need to know where to set up for corner kicks and walls.

The following is an outline of a typical training session for a goalkeeper.

1. *Warm-up.* This part lasts 15 to 20 minutes. Emphasize giving work to the keeper that he does well. This gives him confidence in what he is doing. Various activities can be tried by the keeper. As he begins to tire, he should be instructed to jog slowly to the corner and

Diagram 15-5

back a few times. This will give him a chance to recover and provide a
break in the routine. (See Diagram 15-5.) Some activities can be:

    a. Hand transfer of ball between legs.

    b. Lay flat and execute feet to hands transfer of ball; then reverse
       direction.

    c. Face down, bounce the ball with extended hands.

    d. Seated, legs extended, roll the ball around the body.

    e. Seated, catch served air balls.

    2. *Catching*. Now the keeper is ready to catch balls as outlined
previously: on ground and in the air, short and long, easy and then
hard, left and right.

    3. *Movement*. Construct a small triangular goal with cones/corner
flags about 4 yards to a side. Three attackers are placed, one in front of
each open side to the goal, about 12 yards back. The attackers interpass
a ball until one can shoot. By movement *around* the three cones/corner
flags, the keeper protects the goal and stops the shot. See Diagram
15-6.

Diagram 15-6

    4. *Reaction*. To force the keeper to react quickly, the following
drills can be used:

    a. Place the keeper on the goal line with his *back* to the field. From
       about 15 yards out shoot at the keeper. He may turn when he has

heard the ball being kicked. The angle and distance can be changed as the keeper makes stronger responses.

b. Now the keeper stands with his back to the field, but with both hands on the post. He turns and collects balls as they are struck. It is important to practice this exercise with both goal posts.

c. A group of about five players dribble and pass a ball in front of the goalmouth. While they are doing this, shots are being taken by another player at the edge of the penalty area. The keeper must be alert to spot the ball coming in through the crowd in front of the goalmouth.

5. *Functional.* Two attackers try to score against the keeper and one defender. The attackers are allowed one-touch shots. The defender moves only under the direction of the keeper. The defender must be coached to respond only to verbal commands of the keeper.

While this particular practice ended at this point, there are other elements to be considered. Some to be practiced are:

● quick distribution after the ball is possessed
● punting to target men
● initiating the buildup
● throwing the ball
● teamwork with the libero

It is also worthwhile to give the keeper field practice, as he may assume the role of a field player, as demonstrated in the section on the offside trap.

While the position of the goalkeeper is unique and his training tends to be functional, he must also be considered part of the team. Therefore, part of his training must be done with the team. He must be prepared to be a field player.

Chapter Sixteen

Set Plays

THERE ARE MANY FACTORS to consider in creating set plays. The following is a list of some of these factors.

    A. *Rules*. How do the rules help or hurt the play? As an example, there is no offside rule on the corner kick. How will this affect the first kick? The second touch?

    B. *Score*. Who is winning? By how much? A close game will call for a different response than a game that has become lopsided.

    C. *Time left in game*. How much time is left? This will affect how quickly the play is executed, plus the pace of execution.

    D. *Organization*. What is the system of play? Some teams use four marking fullbacks; others use a sweeper. Players are positioned differently against marking defenders than against a sweeper. Movement is also different.

    E. *Quality of players*. Who has the better team? By how much? There should be a different play against a stronger team than a weaker team.

    F. *Field*. What is the condition of the field? Wet? Dry? Bumps? Long grass? No grass? There must be different plays for different fields. Whose field? Home game or away?

    G. *Weather*. Clear weather? Raining? Is the wind blowing? The wind alone will have a very strong affect on a set play.

    H. *Total environment*. The crowd, the weather, the field, and other elements ... hostile? Friendly?

All of these factors should be considered. The team must have options for each set play and must be highly flexible. As the season progresses, it may be necessary to change the plays. Change is a dominant factor in set plays.

With the above elements in mind, let's review the various restart situations.

The kickoff

For an initial kickoff to start the game or the second half, the best approach is to play a pass forward followed by a back pass to an outside midfield player. From here a normal buildup can be initiated. In starting the buildup from midfield, the attacking team should avoid back passing to the keeper. Ball possession is a primary objective, but not at the expense of retreating to the goal line. Sometimes crossing from one side to the other side is more effective than back passing, as in Diagram 16-1

Diagram 16-1

If the kickoff is a restart following a goal, it is best that the attacking team does just that—attacks. Here the short pass forward is followed by a long pass over one of the wings!

When a team has just scored a goal, the last thing that the players expect is an immediate counterattack. Quickness is the essence of the counterattack.

Since the intention is to move forward, the midfield and fullback lines should be pushed up closer to midfield. On the back pass, the wings can pinch into the middle to create outside space for a fullback to run through. The wings can go wide. Then the fullback can take a square pass and hit the wing with a long pass.

If the ball is played back to the libero, the outside halfbacks run to the top of the box to receive a long pass. Both halfbacks make the runs. All of the above must be done quickly.

Defense of kickoff. The defending team assumes a normal lineup. The center halfback joins the center forward at the top of the circle. When the ball is kicked, the defenders pick up their ordinary (proper) opponents ... fullbacks pick up forwards ... don't let the wings go through! The two center defenders at the top of the circle press ahead—one goes straight forward, down the middle of the field—the second chases to mark the nearest available halfback. This is in anticipation of the back pass to the nearby halfback. It also forces the ball to the side—less danger in the attack.

Direct/Indirect

At midfield the restart must accomplish two objectives. First, it must be executed quickly so that the defenders do not have a chance to organize. (Good advice for *any* part of the field.) Second, it must give the attacking team ball possession so that the attack can be sustained. Often, a square pass to the opposite side will accomplish this. A *short* pass will also help to maintain ball possession. As a last choice, a back pass can be executed.

When the direct/indirect kick is to be taken close to the goal, the opponents will set up a wall—the most common defensive tactic.

The first time the wall is set up it must be attacked with a *hard shot* right at the head of the man covering the near post. Why? If the man ducks, the keeper has the greatest distance to cover to stop the shot. If the wall holds, the attitude of the wall men will be altered. Attacking the flanks will be easier, as the wall players' response is now predictable; they will try to hold *firm* on the wall.

Attacking the wall the second time requires a grouping of five players.

Two variations are shown in Diagrams 16-2A and 16-2B. The first is created by a cluster of three players near the ball with one more wide on each side. From the cluster of three, the two outside players run at the wall in a crisscross pattern. The middle player passes to the open man or chips the ball over the top.

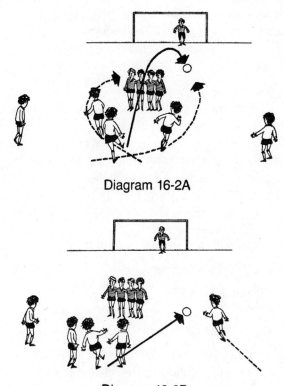

Diagram 16-2A

Diagram 16-2B

In the second variation the middle man passes to an outside player before the crisscross is run. Then a short pass to an open player can be delivered, or a cross to the opposite side of the wall.

Variations can be created by any coach depending on the strength or weakness of his players. A strong team has more variations in attacking the wall than a weak team. Any team that becomes predictable is easier to defend against than one that keeps trying new plays. Back passing by attackers causes uncertainty on the part of defenders, as they are unsure whether they should hold their positions to maintain the wall, or chase after the ball.

Defense. The wall must be set up with an extra player covering the near post side. A forward should direct the positioning of the wall, not the goalkeeper. We have seen two goals scored this past season while the keeper stood at the near post setting up a wall. A forward can stand *behind* the ball, the legal distance away, and set up the wall including the overlapping of the near post. While this is being done, the keeper gets into proper position to protect the goal from a quick restart. When the ball is touched, the wall must either move at the ball as a unit, or break up to mark individual attackers. This must be determined in advance.

Delay is a defender's weapon. How to delay? Set up the wall a *little* short of 10 years, but beware of yellow cards. Also, leave the defender who fouled standing where he fouled. He can hold the ball and hand it to his opponent when he approaches to kick the ball. Don't kick *away* the ball. Defenders who walk back to make a wall will often find the ball ahead of them. They must fall back rapidly, *facing* the ball.

Corner kicks

Let us begin with the normal possibilities:

1. Long ball to the near post
2. Long ball to the far post
3. *Hard* cross either below the knees or to a head
4. Short (Watch out for the offside trap!)

Next, consider the *basic* placement of attackers. The two basic formations are the open echelon and the closed echelon. (See Diagrams 16-3A and 16-3B.) Both require three players in the penalty area, with support players waiting behind in the open field. The more the box is packed with players, the less is the chance to score. Attackers need space to score.

Either an inswinger or outswinger pass may be delivered from the corner to either echelon. The inswinger should be delivered to the near post/near player in the closed echelon; in the open echelon the inswinger goes to or beyond the far post where the "near" man is waiting. In the closed echelon, the outswinger goes to the far post or back position in the echelon; the outswinger goes to the near man in the open echelon. Movement and second touches must be planned on a local level. The prime objective is to have a shot or header follow the

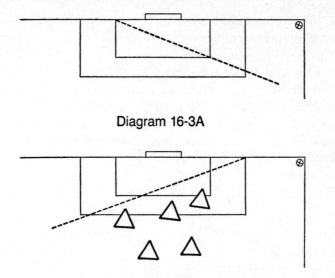

Diagram 16-3A

Diagram 16-3B

corner kick. The best that you can do is *place* the players in the right situation. One other formation is popular with the English and gives them an opportunity to move *back* or forward to the ball. The best corner kicks are the ones that are the *least* complicated and *cluttered*. See Diagram 16-4.

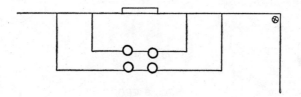

Diagram 16-4

The short corner has many uses:

1. It can be used for surprise.
2. It can take advantage of poor defensive positioning.
3. It can take advantage of an unmarked player.
4. It works well on a wet field.
5. It works well against strong heading teams.

The second player must be close to the goal line so that the first passer is not trapped offside. A good player can fake the straight run to the near post, turn, and move.

Defending against the corner kick must be well planned. The wing should drop back to defend against the short corner (Diagram 16-5). Three defenders should cover the goalmouth: the keeper, slightly off the goaline, a fullback tight on the near post, and one a step or two off the back post. Then, any attackers entering the penalty area must be marked.

Diagram 16-5

A favorite trick is to place a good heading attacker short of the near post. He then back-heads across the goalmouth. The defender on the near post must be ready for this situation. The near-post header is run from the open echelon. (See Diagram 16-6). Some teams like the heading targets to stand still, and others look for movement. Both spell danger.

Local conditions will dictate how set plays are organized. As a final thought, more and more attention is being paid to set plays in Europe. The set plays provide opportunities for scoring goals; they require serious attention, repetition in practice (often!), concentration, and the respect that they deserve.

Diagram 16-6

The Offside Trap

Picture the members of a primitive village hunting for a lion. The able-bodied villagers are in the heavy undergrowth, weapons in hand, seeking to kill the lion. Far away, forming a huge semicircle, the less able of the village create noise and confusion to drive the lion into the area where the armed villagers are waiting. As the line of villagers moves forward chasing the lion, an occasional small animal will burst from the undergrowth and escape between two villagers. The villagers must be disciplined to ignore the small game, *since it is the lion that they are after.*

By analogy, this is how the offside trap should be run. The *purpose* is to win the ball. To serve this purpose, pressure should be put on the player with the ball. While this pressure is being applied, the defenders should begin to move toward midfield and at the player with the ball. If the pressure on the ball player is decreased, the line of defenders stops. When pressure is reapplied, the line again moves toward him. Such a moving line will trap attackers offside; but the purpose is to apply enough pressure to the ball player so that the ball is won from him by a turnover, a bad pass, a misdribble, or just stripped from him.

Which is better, to win the ball at the point where a player is trapped offside, or further upfield closer to the opponent's goal, where a player gave up the ball during intense play? The answer is obvious.

The trap begins with any ball that is carried on an angle away from the goal (a back angle) by passing, heading or whatever, *by a player from either team.*

The other factor is *pressure*. The player receiving the ball must be placed under pressure at once! Ideally, the pressure must increase until he turns over the ball.

If the defensive unit wins the ball, then it must be carried downfield in a counterattack. The players who converged on the ball form a support wall as they race downfield isolating the ball from the rapidly retreating opponents. The objective is to reach midfield, sealing in the ball and the attack on one-half of the field.

While in Holland, we saw an international game in which both teams applied the offside trap at the same time. Both teams had all players rushing toward midfield; for a moment, there were two lines of players, with each line about 10 yards from midfield. In that 20-yards space, the remaining players struggled to gain possession of the ball. It was a fantastic sight!

The Dutch teams *trap* players boldly, loudly, and repeatedly. They seek the ball. They pursue the ball, barely glancing back at the trapped attackers.

How to escape the trap?

The player with the ball must get rid of the pressure, which is usually caused by close marking by opponents who are blocking passing angles. The player under pressure:

1. Square passes to a free teammate
2. Dribbles forward with the ball
3. Crosses the ball to the opposite side of the field

The trap will not work unless it is *clearly* explained and then practiced. The players must have faith and fortitude. It must be initiated with absolute confidence.

Where the trap fails, the teams are often unsure and timid. This dooms the trap to failure. It is not designed for the faint of heart.

Once a team uses the offside trap with confidence, it will be an automatic and valuable tactical weapon. Further coaching will not be necessary. In fact, the trap will be viewed as a *simple* and effective device.

Let's conclude with an example. In Diagram 16-7, attacker #8 has crossed the ball to the left, where it is headed out to attacker #6. The trap is called. Defender #3 moves directly at #6. Defender #6, as the closer one, puts pressure on the ball. The remaining defenders cross the "face" of the man they are marking and then move against #6. Thus, defender #2 cuts off #11 from receiving a pass. Defender #5 isolates #10 (#8 is blocked anyhow). All now converge on the ball.

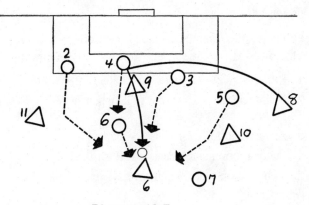

Diagram 16-7

To review: On signal—

Defenders run over the opponent's position.

The ball is placed and kept under pressure.

The ball must not be allowed to be passed ahead.

The line moves to midfield.

Finally, the goalkeeper must come to the top of the box. Here he assumes the position of the libero in the event that the trap fails. (In Holland the keeper often leaves the penalty area and goes 10 or 15 yards into the field. He can play libero there.) The keeper's response will depend on the situation, but he must at least come to the top of the box.

A simple 6 : 4 drill will provide opportunities for running the trap. In a short time, the defensive leader, normally the libero, will need no sideline clues to spring the trap.

A final tip: in the beginning of this handbook the problem of becoming predictable is discussed. The trick with the offside trap is *not* to spring it every time it *can* be sprung. This tends to make the opposition very edgy. (In a recent youth game we advised the referee that we intended to use the offside trap. We wanted him to be prepared for it. He told the other team! So, we never had to run it. The damage had been done. The forwards retreated in anticipation, blunting their own attack.)

The trap is not designed to trap players offside; the trap is designed to win the ball. It is a bold, tactical weapon for bold teams.

Other Set Plays

Other set plays can be created by the coach with suggestions from the team. Several simple factors should be remembered:

1. Restart quickly to prevent the defense from getting set.
2. Maintain ball possession. Your opponents cannot score if you have the ball.
3. At midfield look for wissel—change.
4. Sudden movement signals a call for the ball.
5. Don't become predictable.

Chapter Seventeen

Professional Teams' Practice Sessions

DURING OUR VISITS to Holland we visited professional teams and watched them practice. The first team was the "Go Ahead Eagles" of Deventer. This team is in the first division. It is a semi-pro team; not all of the players train and play full-time for the team. Only four or five teams have a roster of full-time paid professional players. The training program is very different for a professional team and a semi-pro team. The semi-pro team normally has one training session late in the day. Some players arrive late; at Deventer we did not see the full team practice.

Eagles

The practice session observed at Deventer was with a mixture of professionals and semi-pros. We arrived after practice had already begun.

1. The first drill observed was with a long pass from the goal line to midfield. This was the same drill outlined in Chapter Eight, "Combination Finishing Drill." Because of the small number of players, only one side of the field was used, not the two corners as in the previous section. First, ground balls were played, then air balls. The drill finished with a shot on goal, without an opposing defender. See Diagram 17-1.

Diagram 17-1

2. The same as #1, but the passer ran forward to act as the wall player in a one-two combination attack on goal. Again, first ground balls were delivered followed by air balls.

3. A variation of #1 above, but with a defender added in front of the goal. The passer acted as the defender for one sequence, and then moved to midfield. The attacker then became a passer.

4. A stationary player was added to the side to allow the wall pass each time. Then a second stationary player was added to the other side. Now the attacker had the option to wall pass to the left or to the right. (Almost all the finishing shots were on goal. This made the goalkeeper the most active player on the field. There was very little chasing of the ball to the side of the goal, or over the top, as most shots were made directly on goal.)

5. A scrimmage was started with three players on a side, the forwards against defenders. The sweeper could only one-touch the ball.

6. The final scrimmage was five against five on half a field, with one goalkeeper. The forwards again played against the defenders. The defenders attacked an open goal at midfield.

7. The practice session ended with the team practicing penalty kicks. Every drill involved the goalkeeper.

Az '67

The second team we saw was Az '67 of Alkmaar, which is a fully professional team. They practiced twice a day. Special training for goalkeepers or small groups was easy and convenient to organize. The following is an outline of one training session in Alkmaar.

George Kessler (Trainer—Training session with Az '67)
3:30-4:30 (second session of the day)

1. After a warm-up, 3 v 3 with a goalkeeper, the attacking units were rotated against the same three fullbacks. The attackers functioned as forwards trying to work the ball in close to the goal. No long outside shots were taken. There was little wall passing, but takeover ball exchanges were common. The field area used was tight, compressed, and restricted.

2. A sweeper was added to the defense, so that the drill became 3 v 4. The area used was greatly increased compared to step #1 and the emphasis was shifted to wall passes, which placed the ball *behind* the marking defenders. The addition of the sweeper changed the attack to a passing pattern, as opposed to the running of the ball (dribble/takeover) in the man-to-man situation in #1 above.

3. On two-thirds of a field, a scrimmage of 6 v 6 was played. The defense used a sweeper, which created a real 6 v 5 situation in terms of man-to-man marking and using numerical superiority. The emphasis was placed on interplay between the wing and the outside halfback. Kessler pointed out that passes to the opposite wing failed when the wing loudly called for the ball ... "100% failure due to loud calling."

4. The 6 v 6 allowed for a counterattack into a regular goal.

5. A special practice session was run for the two goalkeepers. The training followed the general outline of the section on goalkeeping. Two steps were worth noting:

   a. The ball was played to the same side repeatedly. That is, the shots were not varied from side to side. As the shots were delivered one after the other, the velocity or height was changed little by little. The goalkeeper was challenged to reach farther and farther.

   b. In diving for the ball, the goalkeeper started on the post, not in the middle of the goalmouth. Twenty shots were layed on the ground forcing maximum reach by the goalkeeper. Then the other keeper was placed in the goal for the same drill.

Some observations:

1. Kessler was very concerned with width. He was also concerned with the halfbacks running into space as they ran away from the center

half with the ball. Kessler wanted Peters (right half) to run in the *space* between the right wing and center forward. Then Peters received the ball from the center half.

2. Little crisscross running was observed. Rather, there was a flow, as shown in Figure 17-2. The system of attack was kept in balance, etc., etc.

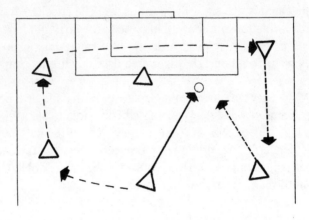

Diagram 17-2

den Hague

The professional team at the Hague was coached by Hans Kraay, who coached Edmonton in the N.A.S.L. His practice was also in a pre-season period.

1. *Warm-up.* The players did static stretching, followed by slow running. They ran along the endline and jumped at the cross bars, simulating heading.

As part of warming up, the players dribbled the ball in a small space. Emphasis was placed on step-over turns, and players were corrected for doing this incorrectly.

Rest intervals wre given, during which the players juggled the ball.

2. *Shooting.* Half the team was drilled in shooting practice. The forwards and midfielders formed a line at the midfield circle. One-by-one they dribbled at the trainer who waited just short of the 18-yard line. The dribbler passed to the trainer who square passed, left or right. The player then took a one-touch shot on goal. Then the line approached from a side. (While this drill was being conducted, the defenders practiced two-man heading.) See Diagram 17-3.

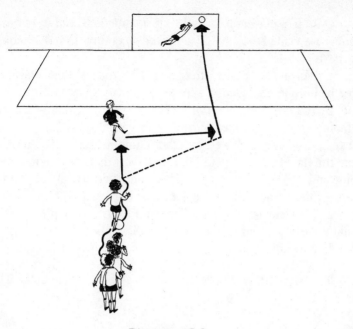

Diagram 17-3

The players practiced shooting with different parts of the foot; instep, outside of the feet, and step-over feints.

3. *Scrimmage*. On half the field, seven attackers played a scrimmage against seven defenders. A keeper defended each goal. The coach called instructions to only the attacker unit.

4. *Shooting*. Now the defenders conducted the same shooting drill as in part 2. The attackers formed 3 : 1 grids. The pace of the 3 : 1 drills was slow.

5. The team was then formed into two groups, and the practice session ended in a full field scrimmage.

Sparta

The final team visited was *Sparta* of Rotterdam. This team is coached by Barry Hughes, an Englishman with a Dutch "A" license. He has lived in Holland for many years and is very popular with the Dutch public. Hughes conducts practice in a combination of Dutch and English commands which the Dutch love. Hughes is a very humorous speaker who peppers his conversation with well-known English expletives.

Only five players have full-time contracts, but all were present on the day we visited. The practice flowed smoothly from one sequence to the next.

1. *Warm-ups*. Static stretching was done by the players. They stretched alone and then in groups of two.

2. *Pass/run combinations*. The players ran three-man pass/run combinations, as outlined earlier in this handbook. The first was the basketball weave, followed by other combinations. The combinations were run the length of the field. The players then walked to the starting point and ran the drill again. This continued for about 15 minutes. Some of the combinations are shown in Figures 17-4A through 17-4D.

3. *Four corner passing*. The team formed four lines, two on the penalty area line and two at midfield. The players passed and rotated from line to line. Four pass/run variations are shown in Figures 17-5A through 17-5D.

This last drill was played with two and then three balls. The pace was rapid.

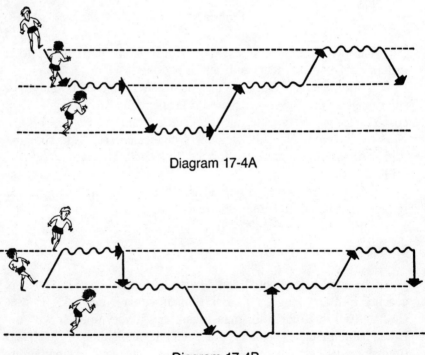

Diagram 17-4A

Diagram 17-4B

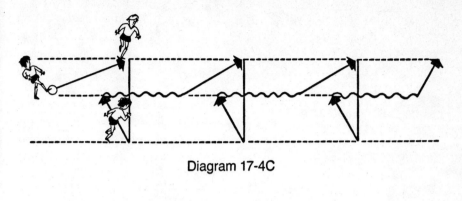

Diagram 17-4C

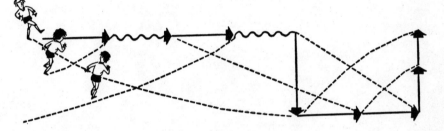

Diagram 17-4D

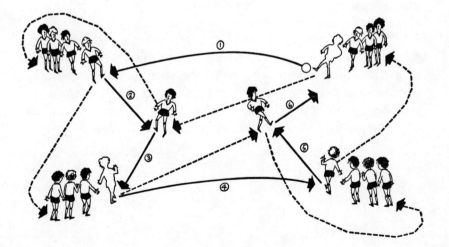

Diagram 17-5A

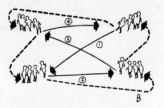

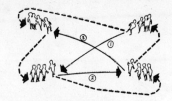

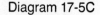

Diagram 17-5B   Diagram 17-5C

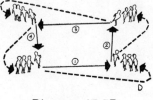

Diagram 17-5D

4. *Scrimmage*. The practice session ended with an 8 : 8 scrimmage on about two-thirds of the field. A portable goal was set up near midfield, but facing in the same direction as the regular goal at the playing end of the field. Hughes explained that this forced long passes and penetrating crosses. He felt that the Dutch game tended to settle into a short passing pattern.

This was a pre-season practice, and there was an exhibition game scheduled for that night. Otherwise, the practice would have been longer and more intense. We noted the poor passing, and Hughes admitted that the team was new to him and needed basic work. The practice was followed by a 45-minute talk on an Englishman's observations of Dutch Voetbal. It was informative and amusing.

Chapter Eighteen

Questions and Answers Asked of the Dutch National Coaching Staff

A *GROUP OF AMERICAN COACHES* was given an opportunity to question the Dutch national coaching staff. Each staff member had an area of responsibility—youth teams, men's amateur, professional. The American coaches asked the staff many questions. Some questions were personal and others were extremely technical. The questions and answers that follow are ones compiled for general interest.

Question: In senior training, assuming that only two weeks are available for pre-season training, what should be stressed?

Answer: If conditioning is 80 percent done, team formation training should be stressed. The following points should be covered:

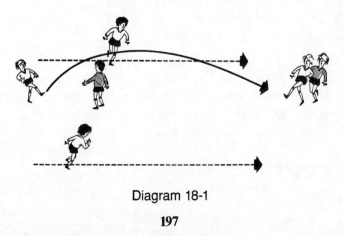

Diagram 18-1

1. Avoid playing less than four on a side in the drill work. This will create the deep pass plays. Less than four aside tends to produce short passing play.

2. Practice 4 v 3 with the backline (fullbacks) making the long pass and running to support and score. Perhaps the attacking part should be 3 v 3.

3. Play 3 v 1 with the long pass ending in 3 v 1. See Diagram 18-1.

4. Do buildup drills with penetration by dribbling, ending in 2 v 1.

5. Don't jump from one drill to another, if they serve the same purpose.

6. Play games of about eight aside, but no more.

7. For a final drill, see Diagrams 18-2A and 18-2B.

Line A player dribbles to midfield and long passes to B. Player B works with upcoming player from line C, creating a 2 v 1 situation, ending the drill with a shot on goal. As a variation, player B runs to midfield and player C runs in to receive the long pass. Finally, player A runs forward after the pass to B, takes a back pass and through passes to C who is moving in from the other side. These points were stressed for short seasons, such as those in most of America.

Question: How about youth soccer in Holland? How is the program organized?

Answer: Six- and seven-year-olds play games of five aside or six aside. Players who are eight or nine play games of seven aside or eight aside. Real competition begins at the age of twelve to fourteen. The goal then is to play 2 games a week or 100 a year. In addition, the teams are encouraged to play in at least three tournments a year. One tournament should be out of the country. At first the emphasis is on technique and tactics. Above the age of fourteen conditioning is added. The teaching emphasis is on technique, tactics and conditioning, including mental conditional training.

Question: How are youth teams trained in Holland?

Answer: Holland is a country of eleven provinces. The Royal Dutch Football Association divides the country into six districts and twenty zones. Each zone runs its own youth development program, and the coaches of these teams must submit weekly reports to national headquarters at Zeist. These reports detail the training program and player development in a particular zone.

Diagram 18-2A

Diagram 18-2B

During the summer each zone sends its teams to Zeist for training by the national staff. During the ten-week period, each zone has one-half a week, or two and one-half days for training. Each district sends a team of 16 players. When all 96 players have been trained, the final selection of a single national youth team is completed.

The training outline is the same for all youth teams:

1. Warm-up
2. Technical exercise (technique)
   a. Demonstrate model
   b. Organize for practice
   c. Train players
   d. Rest with interpassing
3. Technical/tactical—combination drills with player electives (wall pass, give-and-go, etc.)
4. Tactical—introduce a defender
5. End with a game

A specific example of this outline is seen in the actual plans of one of the youth coaches, who wrote the following five-step training outline example for us:

1. *Warm-up:* With several play games
2. *Technique:* Dribbling (with turning-feinting)
3. *Technical/tactical:*
   Dribbling-shooting practice
   Combination forms (wall pass, give-and-go, takeover, etc.)
   Combination forms of shooting on goal
4. *Tactics 4 : 4:* Games with accent on the 1-2 (wall pass) combination and takeovers
5. *Game:* 8 : 8 with the same combination accents over the whole field

These five "headlines," as they are called, are the core of the Dutch youth training program. A variation was also offered for the second session of the day:

1. Warm-up with fitness exercises
2. Power exercises (hopping)—partner exercises
3. Technique training that calls for speed (pace) and control
4. Little games: 2 : 2 and 3 : 3

5. Endurance exercises: With and without the ball
6. Games: 5 : 5 or 6 : 6 with small goals

If two sessions are not held, then the first *five-step* practice is followed.

Player development is slow, sure, and steady. The season is long; the training is continuous. Fields are readily available, and for the participants, this is their only sports activity.

Question: What about heading? How do you teach it?

Answer: We follow the same general outline that we use for training goalkeepers. We begin with the player standing still and practicing basic technique: eyes open, mouth shut, striking the ball with center of the forehead. Once the basic technique is learned, we begin practice with movement:

1. *Running in a circle.* One player heads the ball, and his partner acts as a server. First the running is forward, then backwards.
2. *Jumping.* As in the case of the goalkeeper reaching for high balls, the player now jumps to head high balls. This can be done running forward and then backwards.
3. *Diving.* Again, in a manner similar to the training of a goalkeeper, the player can be taught to head the ball in positions other than standing or jumping. The sequence to follow is:

    a. From a push-up position head the ball
    b. Kneel and head the ball
    c. Squat and head
    d. Crouch and head
    e. Stand and dive (this is a return to the first position—the push-up—but with motion)

Once a player has been trained through this sequence, there should not be any fear of heading a given ball. From this point on the heading work can be integrated with regular soccer practice.

Question: What is the Dutch professional season like?

Answer: I will respond by outlining the season for a first division team. The season begins in July and ends in May. The players are free for the month of June. (Second division teams are free for six weeks.) For the holiday period the players should spend the first two weeks doing other sports: swimming, bicycle riding, etc. Then after two weeks, they start running and do work with the ball.

1. *Club training*. The season begins with a physical examination, weigh-in, and endurance testing. The Cooper test is used for endurance testing. In twelve minutes the field players are to run 3,600 meters, and the goalkeepers to run 2,200 meters. Initial work begins with dribbling and driving of the ball.

Talk to the players and set expectations for the individual, and for the team. Outline and discuss the season's program.

2. *Pre-seasonal*. The pre-seasonal work can be four, six, or even eight weeks long. The emphasis is on technical, tactical, conditional, and mental. Initial work is on the conditional.

Conditional work includes:

a. Endurance—run courses that incorporate Fartlek and Parcourse programs.

b. Speed—After the first two weeks conduct wind sprints.

c. Power—Use the medicine ball and weights if available.

d. Coordination—End each practice with small games, such as five aside; demand personal marking.

e. Shooting—Place ten balls in a line. Shoot one, then run around a post and shoot the next, etc. Time the whole routine for *quickness*.

3. *The season*. The season has two parts, divided by the bad winter weather. For each half specific expectations are set. The evaluation of the first half is based on meeting these expectations, and on what changes must be made for the second half. Will injuries force a change of tactics? Did the opposition play as expected? What must be adjusted for the second half?

4. *Training schedule*. A typical week would follow this schedule:

Saturday — The game

Sunday — Total rest

Monday — Running in the morning

Tuesday — Regular training—two sessions; one in the morning and a second beginning at mid-afternoon

Wednesday — Total rest

Thursday — Regular training (two sessions)

Friday — Regular training (one session)

Saturday — Perhaps a light training session in the morning

5. *A typical session.*

    A. Warm-up - A slow run is followed by flexibilities for 10-15 minutes.

    B. Tactical drills—1 : 1, 2 : 1, combination play 15 minutes.

    C. Tactical/conditional drills for 30 minutes.

    D. Game—play 7 : 7 with accents placed in the game from the above drill work.

    E. Taper off—5 minutes.

As a final comment, it was obvious in watching the professionals train that all players were engaged in some activity at all times. Also, the goalkeepers were active in all drills. None sat and watched; there were no long lines; many balls were needed to sustain the pace.

Question: What is total football?

Answer: Total football means the total integration of the technical, tactical and conditional aspects of the game. All drills/exercises are integrated; conditioning work, as an example, is done with the ball. All players are trained the same way, not by position. Even the goalkeeper is given the basic work, as he is called upon to function as a sweeper on certain occasions.

The elements of total football are:

1. *Freedom.* Every player is free to take any of a variety of options within the team formation.

2. *Rotation.* The various lines—defense, midfield, forward—can overlap. When players rotate positions, this is called rotation soccer.

3. *Takeovers.* Every player must be prepared and willing to take the ball over the position of any other player.

4. *Conditioning.* All players must be in superior condition.

5. *Pressing.* The team must press forward on the attack and must press forward when the ball is lost. (*Pressing football* is the phrase used by Rinus Michels. *Total football* is the popular phrase used by sports journalists.)

6. *Risk.* With the above elements, it should be obvious that the team employing total football must take risks.

The modern game of soccer is really a variation of *total football.* The modern player is in far better condition than the general condition of players 20 years ago. The technique of the individual player is developed in such a way that he is highly capable of changing positions with any other player on the team. As an example, the goalkeeper must be capable of assuming the position of libero, a fullback can overlap and become a wing.

Any training manual that has drills for players by position is not a total football manual. Players must be trained in a fluid, integrated way that goes beyond a single position or system of play.

Question: What is the didactic approach to training?

Answer: We begin by establishing a *purpose* for the practice. One headline or general purpose will serve well, perhaps two or three at most. (A headline could be an emphasis on one factor—wall passing, for example.) Next, we consider the *organization* needed for practice. There are many organizations that can be considered.

  a. Single line
  b. Double row
  c. Circle
  d. Grid or square (including a three cornered grid)
  e. Free organization

Then we list the *choice of practice matters*. This would be the technique, such as push passing, followed by the technical/tactical, such as wall passing.

The *execution* of the drills is then planned. In part, this may be determined by the number of players available for a given drill.

Next, the *method* is reviewed. A demonstration should be given for this. We say, "Show it—tell it—do it." The Germans say:

  1. Demonstrate
  2. Practice
  3. Make automatic
  4. Put in game

Finally, the *variation of possibilities* should be considered. A player mut be made aware of the variation of possibilities available. As an example, in dribbling he must become aware of the many ways of beating an opponent: feinting, turning, combination play. The more that possibilities are identified and practiced, the more a player will use them.

Chapter Nineteen

Match Analysis

TYPICALLY, when watching a soccer game, a Dutch coach will take pen and some paper to keep careful notes on the game. However, his notes are not like those found in a score book. Common statistics are ignored. Assists are not given to goals scored. The exact number of corner kicks and throw-ins is not recorded.

What kinds of notes does he take? What is the purpose? Can we benefit from this approach? What, exactly, does the coach do?

An outline of the field play is used to diagram the position and movement of each player. On the first piece of paper, the position and movement of the fullbacks are recorded. Consideration is given to the formation when the ball has been lost and when the ball has been won. A line indicates how far each player is willing to run upfield. The strongest defender is noted; also the weakest.

The second piece of paper is for recording the same kind of information about the midfield players ... how many ... attacking and defending ... movement ... strong/weak points. A third piece of paper records the activity of the forwards.

The observer normally follows the action of one team, not both teams. First, he records the fullbacks, then midfield, and finally the forwards. When all of this information has been recorded, a fourth sheet is used as a summary of the whole team.

Some other points that these coaches watch for are:

1. *Covering*. Is the defensive team marking man-to-man? Do they zone mark away from the goal? Does the sweeper switch with the stopper? When the ball is lost, how defensive-minded are the front line attackers? The Germans tend to mark man-to-man over the whole field, while the Dutch move man-to-man only in the last 22 yards.

2. *Getting free*. Who is getting free? How? Long runs to the other side? Short, sudden bursts? Overlapping? Switching? Defenders love to mark attackers who run downfield, and then turn, with their backs to the goal, watching the movement of the ball. The modern team attacks the goal with a variety of player moves and sudden changes of speed. Space and pace.

3. *Buildup*. Is the attack being built up from the back? How is the breakout accomplished? Who is delivering the long pass? How does the keeper react under pressure?

4. *Closing lines*. If the defense against the buildup fails, do the players fall back to midfield? This is called closing lines. Many teams have forwards who stop pressuring as soon as the ball is passed out of their area. They *should* fall back to continue to be of help.

5. *The offside trap*. Is the offside trap being used? Does the other team know how to combat the trap?

6. *Set plays*. Finally, the teams must be watched for the execution of set plays.Again, as a generalization, the team that has the most amount of meaningful movement should control the game and its outcome.

Let's review the match analysis of several games. Not every element will be covered, but the basic notes will explain how the analysis is developed. Each coach must learn to develop his own match analysis style. Player movement is normally shown by dotted line. The longer the line, the more often that runs are made in that direction.

Game 1

This was a game between two first division Dutch teams. Both teams were using young, inexperienced players.

The red team set up in a 4-3-3 formation, with player #6 being the sweeper as in Diagram 19-1. (Sometimes this is called the 1-3-3-3 formation.) On the attack this formation changed.The sweeper, #6, and the stopper, #18, made long runs with the ball. This changed the

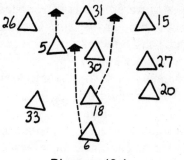

Diagram 19-1

attack formation to 3-4-3, or even 3-4-4. Midfielder #5 ran up between #26 and #31 to become the fourth attacker.

Other than the movement of these players the red team showed very little imagination in attack and had a conventional defense.

The green team was much more imaginative and worthy of more attention and analysis.The team formation was 4-4-2 on defense and 3-4-3 on the attack (see Diagram 19-2). On occasions the attack formation was 3-3-4. (Due to the fluid role of the midfielders in supporting the forwards, it is often difficult to determine the exact number of players in each line. In match analysis, the types of formations are given only to show the willingness of players to change position, support the attack, and challenge the defense. Recognizing such movement is much more important than seeking an exact diagram of team formation.)

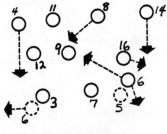

Diagram 19-2

Player #8 set up as a sweeper, but ran forward to become a fourth marking fullback. He also moved into a midfield position. Wing fullbacks #4 and #14 made long runs on their respective sides of the field. The runs by #14 were more effective because #6 withdrew to create space for #14 to run into. When #14 did not make the run into the space, #16 did.Thus, green not only showed four attackers, it showed four *different* attackers.

While #6 withdrew inside to give outside space to either #16 or #14, the wing on the other side, #3, ran outside to create space inside and closer to the goal. The wings often switched, and are shown in dotted figures to illustrate this fact. The green team won the game, and the dotted lines on the diagram give clear reason why this was so.

Game 2

The *second game* was an international one between a Dutch team and a German team.

The Dutch team formation was a 4-3-3. (See Diagram 19-3.) The wing fullbacks #20 and #33 made long runs, normally on the side opposite to the ball. These runs placed an extra attacker on the blind side of the defenders. The wings, #15 and #26, frequently switched sides. This created space for the overlapping fullbacks and prevented the defenders from becoming highly organized.

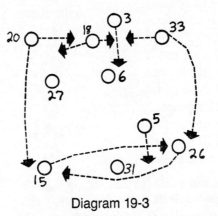

Diagram 19-3

The one key player who did not have enough movement was #31, the center forward. He simply stationed himself in front of the goal as a fixed target for passing. When the ball was lost, he failed to help defensively. The Dutch team was handicapped on the attack and in defense.

The German team also used a 4-3-3 formation. (See Diagram 19-4.) This team had much more movement beginning with the center forward, #9, who withdrew from his position creating space that was used by the two wings #7 and #11, and space that was also used by the outside midfield players.

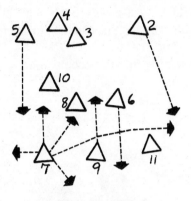

Diagram 19-4

Player #7 created special problems. He withdrew to give space for the overlapping fullback, #5. He also moved outside to create space for #10, a midfielder who ran inside at the goal. Finally, #7 switched sides with #11, the left wing. The wide ranging movements were not unexpected, as was an international star who had been the European player of the year.

Because of the superior movement of the German team and the defensive problems created by #7, the Dutch lost the game. The game could have been closer if the Dutch center forward, #31, had done more than stand in front of the goal.

To review the elements of a match analysis:

1. Diagram the team's formation. Then indicate how they actually operate and systems of play.
2. Note the differences between the two teams:
   a. Covering on defense
   b. Getting free on the attack
   c. Building up
   d. Closing lines defensively
   e. Using the offside trap
   f. The strongest player of each line

g. The weakest player of each line

h. The best player overall

This method will help a coach or a spectator "see" the game more clearly. It is an excellent way to scout a team. At first it will be difficult to concentrate on making adequate notes, but it will become easier after just a few games. In the beginning it is suggested that the match analysis be done by a *group*. Each member of the group can make a post-game contribution that can help to sharpen the analysis for the remaining members.

With a little practice, it will become an easy routine.

Summary

As we write these final words, two thoughts linger. Rinus Michels has gone back to Europe, but his comments remain—15 years to go for America to *become* competitive in world soccer.

We are not offering solutions to the problem or problems, as complex as they tend to become. However, the Dutch have a proverb, "Een goed begin is het halve werk." In plain English, "A good beginning is half the work." This is what we would like to offer—a *good beginning*. We would not be so presumptuous as to offer final solutions, the last word, or the ultimate authority on soccer. But we do believe that we have provided a *good beginning*.

Let us look in summary at some of these elements of a good beginning:

1. We have outlined *technique* with the ball, alone and in groups, with movement and change of pace. To get the game going at a higher level we must move beyond the level of standing to pass-trap the ball. We skipped over that level on purpose. All technique work was done with movement. Players cannot afford the time to stand and watch things happen; they must make things happen by their action; they must *force* things to happen by their actions.

2. *Tactics* begins with choice. We tried to expand that choice of electives up to available electives of a first division professional team. The *awareness* of such electives will help individual coaches and their players to raise the level of their own game, even at the amateur level of competition.

3. *Conditioning* is a necessary and obvious element of any soccer training program that also has *movement*. With older players, pre-season training may contain specific conditioning work, but the normal approach is to combine conditioning with technique or with technical/tactical work.

4. *Mentality* is an element of European soccer that is frequently ignored. We often see the elements of soccer listed as: technique—tactics—conditioning. Period. But mentality is an element—in training, pre-game, half-time, and *basic* to the growth of the individual player. What are we trying to do? Why?

We have tried to make this an underlying theme. We have made this clear in our attitude about goalkeeper training and team tactics. You must get used to the idea of telling your players not only *what* to do but *why*.

211

5. *Freedom*—European soccer gives players freedom—options—that are available to a higher degree to the more skillful player. Players must become aware of the fact that high skill level means more freedom. This gives incentive to become more skillful. This same freedom is available to the more knowledgeable coach. Think about it.

Finally, we have offered *samples* of a training program, set, plays, and a host of options needed by coaches. We have tried not to be dogmatic in offering a complete, closed system of play in soccer; it is doubtful that such a system exists or could ever exist.

In summary, what have we offered?

Een goed begin!

Index